S0-ARL-507

TIMELINE

1680	Father Louis Hennepin visits and names the Falls of St. Anthony
1805	Lieutenant Zebulon Pike negotiates a treaty with the Dakota, who cede territory that includes St. Anthony Falls
1820–23	Colonel Josiah Snelling oversees construction of Fort Snelling and the first mills at the falls
1820–57	The falls area is a tourist attraction, drawing visitors from the eastern United States and Europe
1838	Franklin Steele claims land on east side of falls
1848–87	"Sawdust Town": Minneapolis leads the nation in saw milling
1854–55	First bridge across the Mississippi River constructed
1855	St. Anthony incorporated; Congressman Robert Smith buys land on west side of falls
1856	Minneapolis Mill Company and St. Anthony Falls Water Power Company incorporated
1856–58	Companies construct a dam to funnel water to each side of the river
1858	Minnesota becomes a state
1867	Minneapolis incorporated
1869	Tunnel collapse on east side threatens falls
1870–84	The falls is restored and protected by an apron, dam, and dike
1870s	"New process" revolutionizes the flour milling industry
1872	St. Anthony and Minneapolis merge into one city
1878	Washburn A mill explodes, killing eighteen workers and destroying much of the west side mill district
1880–1930	"Mill City": Minneapolis leads the nation in flour production
1882	The nation's first hydroelectric plant begins operating on Upton Island
1883	Stone Arch Bridge opens to rail travel
1897	The Lower Dam hydroelectric plant is built and leased to the Twin City Rapid Transit Company
1904	The last sawmill located at the falls shuts down
1920	Saw milling above the falls draws to a close
1930–50	Many flour mills are dismantled; bridges and railroad trestles are cleared from the district
1950–56	Lock and dam construction opens the upper river to navigation
1957	Northern States Power becomes the sole licensee of waterpower at the falls
1959–63	Second lock and dam constructed
1965	Washburn A mill closes
1971	St. Anthony Falls Historic District listed on the National Register of Historic Places
1996	St. Anthony Falls Heritage Trail opens
2001	Mill Ruins Park opens
2003	Mill City Museum opens

MILL CITY

Visiting

THE FALLS

First Views

The Mississippi River winds 2,200 miles from its source in Minnesota's Lake Itasca to the Gulf of Mexico. What we today know as the Falls of St. Anthony is the only significant waterfall along the river's course. Small wonder that this sixteen-foot drop was noted prominently in the journals and published accounts of North America's explorers. The first European to see the falls was Father Louis Hennepin, and he named it in honor of the patron saint of travelers. Later explorers praised the cataract's picturesque beauty but little imagined the changes that would take place as people harnessed its waterpower.

~~~~~~

Father Louis Hennepin was a Franciscan priest who in 1680 traveled along the upper Mississippi at the request of the French explorer La Salle. Hennepin and his party were captured by a band of Dakota and held near Mille Lacs Lake for two months before securing permission to travel to the Wisconsin River for supplies. During this leg of the journey, the Dakota showed Father Hennepin the falls, a site of spiritual significance. A published narrative of his travels, titled *Description of Louisiana*, included an exaggerated account of the waterfall's height and power, and from this first word its fame would only spread.

> *I named it the Falls of St. Anthony of Padua in gratitude for favors God did me through the intercession of that great saint, whom we chose as patron and protector of all our enterprises. The waterfall is forty or fifty feet high and has a small rocky island, shaped like a pyramid, in the center.*
>
> *While portaging our canoe at the Falls of St. Anthony of Padua, we caught sight of five or six of our Indians who had set out before us. One of them had climbed an oak across from the large waterfall and was weeping bitterly. He had a beaver robe dressed neatly, whitened inside, and decorated with porcupine quills, and was offering it in sacrifice to this cataract, which is terrifying and admirable. I heard what he was saying to it while weeping bitterly: "You, who are a spirit, grant that our tribe pass by here tranquilly without mishap. Grant that we may kill many buffaloes, destroy our enemies, and bring here captives, some of whom we will sacrifice to you."*

Father Hennepin blesses and names the falls and several Indians observe the ceremony
with nonchalance in this stylized depiction by Douglas Volk.

Jonathan Carver was an adventurer from Connecticut who explored North America in
the 1760s. Directed by Major Robert Rogers, who sought the elusive Northwest Passage,
Carver mapped parts of present-day Wisconsin, Illinois, and Minnesota. His account,
Travels through the Interior Parts of North America, the first popular American travel book,
depicted the falls in detail.

> *We could distinctly hear the noise of the water full fifteen miles before we reached
> the Falls; and I was greatly pleased and surprised, when I approached this astonish-
> ing work of nature.*
>
> *This amazing body of waters, which are above 250 yards over, form a most
> pleasing cataract; they fall perpendicularly about thirty feet, and the rapids below, in
> the space of 300 yards more, render the descent considerably greater; so that when
> viewed at a distance they appear to be much higher than they really are. [Father
> Hennepin] has laid them down at above sixty feet; but he has made a greater error
> in calculating the height of the Falls of Niagara; which he asserts to be 600 feet;
> whereas from latter observations accurately made, it is well known that it does not
> exceed 140 feet. But the good father I fear too often had no other foundation for his
> accounts than report, or, at best, a slight inspection.*

In the middle of the Falls stands a small island, about forty feet broad and somewhat longer, on which grow a few cragged hemlock and spruce trees; and about half way between this island and the eastern shore is a rock, lying at the very edge of the Fall, in an oblique position, that appeared to be about five or six feet broad, and thirty or forty long. These Falls vary much from all the others I have seen, as you may approach close to them without finding the least obstruction from any intervening hill or precipice.

The country around them is extremely beautiful. It is not an uninterrupted plain where the eye finds no relief, but composed of many gentle ascents, which in the summer are covered with the finest verdure, and interspersed with little groves, that give a pleasing variety to the prospect. On the whole, when the Falls are included, which may be seen at the distance of four miles, a more pleasing and picturesque view cannot, I believe, be found throughout the universe. I could have wished that I had happened to enjoy this glorious sight at a more seasonable time of the year, whilst the trees and hillocks were clad in nature's gayest livery, as this must have greatly added to the pleasure I received; however, even then it exceeded my warmest expectations. I have endeavored to give the Reader as just an idea of this enchanting spot as possible, in the plan annexed; but all description, whether of the pencil or the pen, must fall infinitely short of the original.

Jonathan Carver's travel account was the first to advertise the upper Northwest to the English-speaking world. His book included descriptions of the natives, a detailed map, and the earliest printed view of the falls. Boats, teepees, and people portaging attest to the fact that the falls was a busy place prior to European settlement.

Major Stephen H. Long explored the upper Mississippi in 1817 to evaluate land ceded in an 1805 treaty negotiated with the Dakota by Lieutenant Zebulon Pike. The territory included a nine-mile-wide band on each side of the Mississippi from the Falls of St. Anthony to the mouth of the Minnesota River, and Long reported to the U.S. government that this area would be well suited as a military reservation. His journal, titled "Voyage in a Six-Oared Skiff to the Falls of St. Anthony in 1817," offered a detailed description of the area surrounding the falls.

> *Tuesday, July 15 About four miles above the mouth of the St. Croix, as it is said, is the narrowest part of the Mississippi below the Falls of St. Anthony. At this place we crossed the river from a dead start, with sixteen strokes of our oars. The river is here probably between one hundred and one hundred and twenty yards wide, but as we had a favorable wind up the river we did not stop to measure it. Upon supposition that the country, on ascending the Mississippi, would lose its alluvial and second- ary character, and exhibit nothing but traits of primitive formations, not only in its precipices but even upon its surface, I had expected to find on this part of the river, not merely bluffs and knolls five or six hundred feet high, but, also, mountains of vast height and magnitude. On the contrary I now discover that we have long since passed the highest lands of the Mississippi and that we are now moving through a rolling prairie country, where the eye is greeted with the view of extensive undu- lating plains, instead of being astonished by the wild gigantic scenery of a world of mountains.*
>
> *The highlands on this part of the river are elevated from one to two hundred feet above the water level. The bluffs are more regular, both in their height and direc- tion, than they are below Lake Pepin, and the valley of the river more uniform in its width. The stratifications of the bluffs are almost entirely sandstone, containing clay and lime in greater or less proportions. The pebbles are a mixture of primitive and secondary stones of various kinds. Blue clay or chalk is frequently to be found.*
>
> *. . . The rapids below the Falls of St. Anthony commence about two miles above the confluence of the Mississippi and St. Peter's [Minnesota River], and are so strong that we could hardly ascend them by rowing, poleing, and sailing, with a strong wind, all at the same time.*

The sandstone bluffs Long described resulted from the falls' retreat over a twelve-thousand- year period. The geology of the falls contributed to this movement: sandstone one hun- dred feet thick was covered by a thin layer of limestone that broke off as the force of the current dissolved its supporting tier. Originally part of Glacial River Warren near present-day St. Paul, the falls reached Mendota ten thousand years ago and split into two, with the Minnesota River side quickly becoming a rapids and the Mississippi side retreating up the gorge. Even after the first explorers viewed the falls, erosion caused it to recede at the rate of two to three feet per year. In part this explains why descriptions of the falls from the 1600s to the 1800s differ significantly.

~~~~~

Major Thomas Forsyth was Indian agent at Rock Island, Illinois, and in 1819 he joined Colonel Henry Leavenworth and his troops as they traveled to the St. Anthony Falls area to build a military post. Later named Fort Snelling, it was the first permanent white settlement in what would become Minnesota. Forsyth kept a diary of the expedition.

> *Saturday, August 28th. I set out early this morning, accompanied by Col. Leavenworth, Major Vose, Dr. Purcell, Lt. Clark and Mrs. Gooding, to visit the Falls of St. Anthony. My boat being strong manned, we made good headway, but the more we approached the Falls, the stronger the rapids became. I left the boat with one man to guard it, and we set out by land, having only a distance of one mile to walk to the Falls. In going out of a thick woods into a small prairie, we had a full view of the Falls from one side to the other, a distance of about four or five hundred yards. The sight to me was beautiful; the white sheet of water falling perpendicularly, as I*

Adolph Hoeffler, who painted St. Anthony Falls in 1849, lamented its uninspired name: "Shall we ever forgive Father Hennepin for hiding the Ojibwe name of *Kakabikah* (severed rock), and the Dakota *Irara* (laugh), beneath the brown mantle of St. Anthony of Padua?"

*should suppose, about twenty feet—but Gen. Pike says he measured and found it
sixteen and a half feet—over the different precipices; in other parts, rolls of water,
at different distances, falling like so many silver cords, while about the island large*

*bodies of water were rushing through
great blocks of rocks, tumbling every
way, as if determined to make war
against anything that dared to approach
them. All this was astonishing to me
who never saw the like before. After viewing the Falls from the prairie for some
time, we approached nearer, and by the
time we got up to the Falls, the noise of
the falling water appeared to me to be
awful. I sat down on the bank and feasted
my eyes, for a considerable time, in viewing the falling waters, and the rushing of
large torrents through and among the
broken and large blocks of rocks, thrown
in every direction by some great convul-*

"St. Anthony [is] one of the most romantick places on the Missippi . . . nature has
done for this place what she has not done for many others viz the river here falls
over the rocks some 20 ft and on both sides for 1½ miles leaves a butiful plain for
building a city." reported William K. McFarlane in "Sketches of Minnasota by
an Emigrant." (Alexis Jean Fournier, *St. Anthony Falls, 1786*, oil, 1887)

*sion of nature. Several of the company crossed over to the island above the Falls, the
water being shallow. The company having returned from the island, they told me
that they had attempted to cross over the channel on the other side of the island, but
the water was too deep, and they say the greatest quantity of water descends on the
other or north-east side of the island. We proceeded to the boat and embarked, and
was down at the encampment at sundown.*

Traveler and student of Indian life **Henry Rowe Schoolcraft** chronicled his 1820 visit to
the falls in *Narrative Journal of Travels through the Northwestern Regions of the United
States, Extending from Detroit through the Great Chain of American Lakes to the Sources of
the Mississippi River, in the Year 1820.* As the book's lengthy title suggests, Schoolcraft
hoped to locate the headwaters of the Mississippi River. In 1832, with the help of local
Ojibwe, he succeeded, naming the river's source Lake Itasca.

*The falls of St. Anthony are fourteen miles below the confluence of the Mississaw-
gaeigon [Rum River]. We reached the upper end of the portage at half past eight
in the morning, and while the voyageurs were busied in the transportation of our*

baggage, hastened to take a view of this celebrated cataract. The river has a perpendicular pitch of forty feet, with a formidable rapid above and below. An island at the brink of the falls, divides the current into two sheets, the largest of which passes on the west of the island. The rapid below the schute is filled with large fragments of rock, in the interstices of which some alluvial soil has accumulated, which nourishes a stinted growth of cedars. This rapid extends half a mile, in which distance the river may be estimated to have a descent of fifteen feet. The rapid preceding the falls, has a descent of about ten feet in the distance of three hundred yards, where the river runs with a swift but unruffled current over a smooth stratum of rock a little inclined towards the brink. The entire fall therefore in a little less than three fourths of a mile,

"The eye embraces at once the view, the copses of oak upon the prairies, and the cedars and pines which characterize the calcareous bluffs. Nothing can exceed the beauty of the prairies which skirt both banks of the river above the falls," praised Henry Rowe Schoolcraft. Henry Lewis's *St. Anthony Falls*, painted in 1900, displayed nostalgia for a nature that had been obliterated by industrialization at the falls.

is sixty-five feet. The rock is a white sand stone overlayed by secondary lime stone. This formation is first seen half a mile above the falls, where it breaks out abruptly on the banks of the river. . . . The scene presents nothing of that majesty and awe which is experienced in the gulf below the cataract of Niagara. We do not hear that deep and appalling tone in the roar of water, nor do we feel that tremulous motion of the rocks under our feet which impresses the visitor at Niagara with an idea of greatness, that its magnificent outline of rock and water, would not, independently, create. The falls of St. Anthony, however, present attractions of a different nature. We see nothing in the view which may not be considered either rude or picturesque, and perhaps there are few scenes in the natural topography of our country, where these features are blended with more harmony and effect. It is in fact the precise point of transition, where the beautiful prairies of the upper Mississippi, are merged in the rugged lime stone bluffs which skirt the banks of the river from that point downward. . . . It is probable, too, that during the high floods of the Mississippi in the spring and fall, this cataract attains a character of sublimity, from the increased volume and tumult of the water, and the inundation of the accumulated debris, which presents, at this season, so rugged an aspect. It is said, also, that this accession of *water produces a cloud of spray which must take away a certain nakedness in the appearance of the falls, that will strike every visitor who has previously enjoyed the sight of the Niagara.*

⌇⌇⌇⌇⌇

As a geologist for the U.S. government, Englishman **George Featherstonhaugh** traveled through some of its remote territories in the 1830s; he was only the second European explorer of the Minnesota River region. In 1846 he published *A Canoe Voyage up the Minnay Sotor,* which also chronicled his surveys for mineral wealth in Wisconsin, Missouri, Georgia, and the Carolinas.

September 14—We had between eight and nine miles to go against the current, which made our progress very slow. The bluffs had the same character with those opposite to Fort Snelling, but diminished in height as we proceeded, being about eighty feet high, coming down to the river with occasional slopes and bottoms of low land, the river averaging about 100 yards in breadth. As we advanced but slowly, we landed on the left bank, and ascending to the top of the bluff, got upon an extensive and beautiful prairie. . . .

Descriptions of the falls differed greatly because the falls themselves were changing. By the 1850s, there were two waterfalls, the west or main waterfall, which is still visible today, and the east face, located between the east shore and Hennepin Island, which is now dammed. (Seth Eastman, engraving, 1854)

After a short walk we came in sight of the Falls of St. Anthony, which perhaps look best at a distance; for although upon drawing near to them they present a very pleasing object, still, from their average height not exceeding perhaps sixteen feet, they appeared less interesting than any of the great cascades I had seen in North America. . . .

The line of the cascade, like that of Niagara, is interrupted by a small island, and, including it, has an irregular curvature of about 650 yards from bank to bank, the river contracting below the falls to about 180 yards. The current above the cascade is very strong, and comes dashing over the fractured limestone of this irregular curvature, where it recedes and advances with great variety of plays, so that in its details this is a cascade of very great beauty, its incessant liveliness contrasting pleasingly with the sombre appearance of the densely wooded island, and presenting to the observer that element in motion which has so much modified the whole channel of the Mississippi.

PHOTOGRAPHY

The falls area has always inspired artistic expression, both in words and pictures. Many sought to capture its essence, and the region's best-known photographers have work represented in this book, from St. Paulites Joel E. Whitney and his protégé Charles A. Zimmerman to regional photographer Benjamin F. Upton and Minneapolitan William Jacoby.

Alexander Hesler took daguerreotype pictures and owned a gallery in Galena, Illinois. As he recounted in a letter to Russell Blakeley, he was joined on one of his trips up the Mississippi by Joel E. Whitney, who would become the region's most famous daguerreotypist.

In 1851, Alexander Hesler photographed the falls looking west from Hennepin Island.

The next summer [1852]—I made arrangements with [Whitney] to join me in making a series of views about St Paul and St Anthony & the surrounding country

August 15th 1852—we left St Paul at 4 a.m. for a day viewing, at 6 a.m. we pitched our viewing tent on Hennepin Island, and began operations Mr Whitney buffing & coating the plates while I selected the views, made the exposures—and developed & fixed the plates. By 10 a.m. we had secured 30 fine views

we were so absorbed in our work, & elated with the scenes that we had taken no thought to the wants of the inner man—but as we were preparing to leave the Island, we stumbled across a small [boy]—who was munching away at a huge "Dough Nut"— Then we were awful!! hungry—and interviewed the young man as to where he procured such a delicasy—To which he replied "Down There" pointing through the Thicket to the lower end of the Island, which was at that time thickly covered with woods & underbrush. —We "Down There" found a squatters cabin in which was a woman busily cooking the said Doughnuts; a large plateful standing on the table these we exchanged for fifty cents, and made for the Ferry above the Falls. The ferry was Propelled as all early settlers will remember by a rope stretched across the river to which the boat or Scow, was attached by ropes & Pullies, and as the forwart part was shortened up & the stern let out, the force of the current propelled the thing along.

On the west side where now stands the Beautiful City of Minneapolis! not a house was to be seen, save a tumble down uninhabited log cabin near the edge of the falls—which site is now covered with those huge flowering mills whose Products feed so many millions.

Excursionists

Once Fort Snelling was established as an outpost and steamboats made Mississippi River travel practical, the falls became a tourist attraction for artists, writers, politicians, and wealthy excursionists. Some came from the east; others from abroad. Many were eager to see the waterfall's native flora and fauna, detailed by those who had preceded them. And many were disappointed to discover that the falls no longer existed in the pristine state described by Hennepin and Carver.

~~~~~

Italian nobleman, political figure, and scholar **Giacomo C. Beltrami** effusively described his 1823 visit to the falls in *A Pilgrimage in America: Leading to the Discovery of the Sources of the Mississippi and Bloody River: With a Description of the Whole Course of the Former and of the Ohio.* The truth of his travels was that he had invited himself to join Major Stephen H. Long's expedition up the Minnesota and Red Rivers. Leaving the group at Pembina, Beltrami sought the source of the Mississippi River, locating and naming Lake Julia, which he incorrectly advertised as the headwaters of the Mississippi and Red Rivers.

> *What a new scene presents itself to my eyes, my dear Madam! How shall I bring it before you without the aid of either painting or poetry? I will give you the best outline I can, and your imagination must fill it up. Seated on the top of an elevated promontory, I see, at half a mile distance, two great masses of water unite at the foot of an island which they encircle, and whose majestic trees deck them with the loveliest hues, in which all the magic play of light and shade are reflected on their brilliant surface. From this point they rush down a rapid descent about two hundred feet long, and, breaking against the scattered rocks which obstruct their passage, they spray up and dash together in a thousand varied forms. They then fall into a transverse basin, in the form of a cradle, and are urged upwards by the force of gravitation against the side of a precipice, which seems to stop them a moment only to encrease the violence with which they fling themselves down a depth of twenty feet. The rocks against which these great volumes of water dash, throw them back in white foam and glittering spray; then, plunging into the cavities which this mighty fall has hollowed, they rush forth again in tumultuous waves, and once more break*

against a great mass of sandstone forming a little island in the midst of their bed,
on which two thick maples spread their shady branches.

A mill and a few little cottages, built by the colonel for the use of the garrison,
and the surrounding country adorned with romantic scenes, complete the magnifi-
cent picture.

Celebrated for his depictions of Indian life, artist **George Catlin** visited the falls and published a sketch of the view in 1841 in his *Letters and Notes on the Manners, Customs, and*
Condition of the North American Indians. He was less impressed with its size and power than
some previous visitors had been.

The Fall of St. Anthony is about nine miles above this Fort, and the junction of the
two rivers; and, although a picturesque and spirited scene, is but a pigmy in size to
Niagara, and other cataracts in our country—the actual perpendicular fall being but
eighteen feet, though of half a mile or so in extent, which is the width of the river;
with brisk and leaping rapids above and below, giving life and spirit to the scene.

George Catlin's staid sketch of St. Anthony Falls left little doubt that
they offered no competition to the majestic falls of Niagara.

～～～～～

A prolific writer and astute observer, **Elizabeth Ellet** took the "fashionable tour" of the Northwest in 1852. In her *Summer Rambles in the West* she noted both the grandeur and the economic potential of the falls.

"The beholder must spend hours on this spot, drinking in its bewildering loveliness, before he can understand how completely the feelings may be subdued into harmony with the scene." Excursionist Elizabeth Ellet encouraged armchair travelers to imagine the falls in their pristine state. (*Harper's New Monthly Magazine*, engraving, 1853)

The site of St. Anthony is a beautiful one; an elevated plateau on the east side of the Mississippi overlooking an extent of prairie. It is about eight miles by land from St. Paul, and at high water is the head of navigation. Its advantages of water power and location will make it one day a great manufacturing place.

It is a pleasant walk or a short drive from the hotel along the river to the falls. A pond on the left of the rapid current is filled with innumerable logs, floated down the river from a distance of several hundred miles, and directed from the current into this reservoir, to be converted into boards in the saw-mill, which is in operation day and night. Above, the rapids extend half a mile—a broad wild waste of tumbling waters bordered by craggy shores, which, when the current is swollen by the spring flood, must present a sight rivaling the celebrated rapids of St. Mary's River. A little below, a foot-bridge two boards wide, shackling and uncertain, but safe enough at the present season, conducts you to an elevated, rocky island, which divides the two principal falls. This island is inhabited, and thickly wooded, and about one hundred yards wide. Crossing it at the upper end to the shore, and descending to a smooth ledge of rock, you come soon to the shelf of rock which faces the great fall of St. Anthony. This is worn by the water into a crescent form, and embraces three separate falls, besides smaller cascades. The perpendicular descent is not more than eighteen feet; but the vast body of water, the force with which it precipitates itself, the curve of the rock, and the wild beauty of the rapids above and below, together with the rush and roar of the waters, lashed into fury by their arrest among the boulders and logs heaped in wildest confusion at the foot of the descent over which they leap, throwing volumes of rainbow-crowned spray into the air, combine to impress the beholder with emotions of awe and admiration.

To view the fall on the other side of the river, it is necessary to recross the foot-bridge and walk up to the larger horse-bridge; then to cross this and go down the hill to the ferry. This is another curiosity—the ferry-boat moving with its burden across the rapid water without the aid of machinery, steam or horse-power. Having reached the opposite shore, walk down the river to the old government mill on the bank, and a fine view is obtained of the tremendous rapids which form the other great fall. The grandeur of the scene grows on the sense, which becomes enlarged as you gaze upon it, to apprehend more and to be filled with a new conception of the greatness of the Creator of all this wondrous magnificence.

Swedish author **Fredrika Bremer** toured the United States in 1849–50, spending a few autumn weeks in the vicinity of St. Anthony Falls. In her immensely popular travelogue *The Homes of the New World: Impressions of America*, she predicted that Minnesota would become "a new Scandinavia."

The Falls of St. Anthony have no considerable height, and strike me merely as the cascade of a great mill-dam. They fall abruptly over a stratum of a tufa rock, which they sometimes break and wash down in great masses. The country around is neither grand, nor particularly picturesque . . . River, falls, country, views, every thing here has more breadth than grandeur.

Fredrika Bremer's account of her travels in Minnesota encouraged Scandinavians to immigrate to this land of great promise.

It was Father Hennepin, the French Jesuit, who first came to these falls, brought hither captive by the Indians. The Indians called the falls "Irrara," or the Laughing Water; he christened them St. Anthony's. I prefer the first name, as being characteristic of the fall, which has rather a cheerful than a dangerous appearance, and the roar of which has nothing terrific in it. . . . Immediately above the falls, it runs so shallow over a vast level surface of rock that people may cross it in carriages, as we did to my astonishment. At no great distance below the falls the river becomes again navigable, and steamers go up as far as Mendota . . . The Falls of St. Anthony are the last youthful adventure of the Mississippi. For nine hundred miles the river flows along the territory of Minnesota, a great part of which is wild and almost unknown country.

~~~~~

Frank Wells visited Minneapolis in 1856 and the next year Knox College published his impressions as "Journey to Minneapolis." He was not the first to express nostalgia for a falls untouched by human endeavors.

The river, as we gain a view of it down in its deep channel, is rolling on a turbulent burden of boiling, frothy eddies; and shoals of long-winded bubbles are all the time coming to the surface, and the low noise of their bursting is scarcely distinguishable from the roar of the rapids and cataract above. On either side of the river we see the villages of St. Anthony and Minneapolis, connected with each other by two long bridges. But I have no admiration for the bridges, nor for the "thriving, beautifully situated, healthfully located" villages. It would better suit my taste if the whole region were as uncivilized as when Father Hennepin was here; although in that case we should have lost the kind reception which we had at a friend's house in Minneapolis.

And now we are crossing the bridge. The water is boiling along under us; and there is a rapid little stream plunging off over the high rocky bank, forming a beautiful cascade. The falls are in sight—the long line of rapids above and below. Much of the beauty of the Falls is covered up by a great pile of logs lodged in drifting down. Near the middle of the river, and a few yards below the falls, is Hennepin Island,

"[The falls] have presumably lost none of their original grandeur and beauty, but the surrounding scenery has changed. The 'beautiful country' is covered with the fine stately buildings of the new and flourishing cities on each side, or cut up into regularly laid out farms," observed visitor John McCoy in 1857. Frank Wells decried this "changed scenery" and the evidence of industry, including logs floated downriver from northern pinelands. (Joel E. Whitney photo, 1851)

*rising thirty or forty feet from the water, exposing bare seamed rock, covered on top
with beautiful trees. The fall is about fifty feet high—broken into all conceivable
shapes. In one place the water strikes in its descent, a rounded stone, and then shoots
off in all directions, making a beautiful convexity like one side of a dome. In hardly
any place is there an uninterrupted descent; it is all foam and flurry. We went down
to the bank after the stage stopped, and where, covered with bushes and trees, it
slopes down to the rocky brink, we walked along, by the aid of bushes and trees,
enjoying the sight and sound.*

～～～～～

World traveler **Johann Georg Kohl** spent four years in America, from 1854 to 1858, and
wrote three books and numerous articles about his sojourn. A geographer, historian, and
scientist, Kohl was also skilled in the literary arts. In his *Travels in the Northwestern United
States* he described the falls in scientific detail and then turned his attention to the damage ensuing from human settlement.

*At last we have reached the famous falls . . . Nature's tool here, the Mississippi,
carved these falls out of two layers: limestone above and beautiful light-colored
sandstone below. In the upper Mississippi Valley a traveler observes this limestone-
sandstone formation anywhere a slope bares itself to the eye, but also along the
Minnesota and St. Croix. Each layer is equally thick everywhere. Any piece broken
off from either is therefore always uniform in structure. The friable sandstone,
much more fragile than the limestone, can sometimes be broken off in pieces with
the fingers. Hence the undermining of rock took place in the sandstone layer and
gave first cause for the creation of a rocky precipice and a waterfall. The water dashing upward wore away the sandstone from below, while, presumably, water from
above found its way through fissures and fractures to the sandstone, washed part
away, and thus induced crumbling and collapse of limestone. These circumstances
produced all the various details now visible. Most prominent are the great pieces of
rock, so remarkably uniform in shape, in great masses along both shores. Here and
there these rocks, almost all of which come in parallelogram shapes, have sometimes been pushed like ice floes into step-like formations.*

*. . . I have now summarized briefly and approximately what I found interesting
about my observation of the falls. The rest was distressing—at least for a friend of
wild and unspoiled nature, of "spirit island," and of magnificent works of creation
that a devotee of nature dedicates to saints. A millwright, a weaver, or a sawyer
might also enjoy what perturbed me; but the spirits and saints have now been driven*

off, the charm sullied. City building and speculation fever, and the archenemies of beauty in our time have taken over here and are gradually turning the lovely haunts of nymphs and mermaids into a very prosaic millpond. The entire vicinity is on the verge of becoming a temple to the gods of manufacture and trade.

"Many falls have so fortified themselves behind boulder and hidden themselves in wilderness that Mistress Improvement just has to leave them in peace. But these falls on the Mississippi are so placed by nature as to seem to have chosen the situation themselves," noted Johann Georg Kohl. Logs and sawmill waste were beginning to choke the falls by the 1850s. (B. F. Upton, photo)

Above the falls a suspension bridge (by the way, the first anywhere across the Mississippi) already swings over the river. Houses, springing up like mushrooms and crowding the falls on both sides, are becoming the city of St. Anthony, friendly and youthful. People want and definitely expect it to be the Manchester or Lowell of the northern Mississippi states. Snarling their threat, lumber barons and other speculators have already seized the beautiful nymphs and mermaids: La vie ou la bourse *[Your money or your life].*

Walls and dams have been built out into the falls, and the goddesses reduced to slaves who work their treadmills. The water being so low, the Mississippi could not carry away the massive load of sawdust, chips, odds and ends of board and plank, and logs dumped in upstream. This industrial waste was stuck everywhere in big jumbled heaps in the falls' attractive little niches and in rocky clefts intended by Nature for the joyous downward passage of crystalline waters. It was a miserable picture, I say, and when I looked at it I believed I saw the good old river god himself before me, powerless, groaning under that excessive load of woody trash that had been dumped on him, shrunken, pitiful, and leaning on his rock.

~~~~~

An author, journalist, and theater director, **Robert Watt** traveled from Denmark to Minnesota in 1871 and later that year published the first of three volumes describing his impressions of America and Canada.

The Falls of St. Anthony in the Mississippi River, which we visited later, at a distance of something like a [Danish] mile from Minne-ha-ha *Falls, are much larger and much more imposing, but the charm that is characteristic of* Minne-ha-ha *they lack altogether. Moreover, a pair of very active factory towns occupy the two banks of the river. The water spirits have been seized by powerful human hands and compelled to turn the wheels in clamorous saw, paper, and flour mills and in large* woolen mills and linen factories. Of course they have rebelled now and then when they have been turned aside with too much boldness from the wild antics with their companions, from their roaring and fuming and their dashing down from the rough rocks to send the foam up from the massive blocks that are thrown in confusion below. Then it has not been possible to tame them to a quiet run and they have cut under the ground and suddenly sent whole factories into the depths. But nevertheless most of them must work. Here is not a question of gracious play as among the nymphs of Minne-ha-ha. It is in a real sense a continuous fight in which the advantage is now with one side, now with the other.

On one side of the falls, where the town of St. Anthony is situated, the waters have done a good deal of damage. We saw ruins of factories lying in the strong current below the falls, and we saw other buildings deserted and surrendered to the fate that awaited them. In Minneapolis, on the other hand, the wheels turn ceaselessly. An entire section of the city consists only of factories built side by side in the immediate vicinity of the falls. Minneapolis continuously vies with St. Paul for the foremost place in the state. If it has lost the honor of being the capital of Minnesota, it can console itself with the fact that it has entirely eclipsed its neighbor, St. Anthony, across the river. St. Anthony gave promise for a time of luxurious growth, but now it has come to a complete standstill and that in spite of the fact that it has the advantage of any city in the state as far as manufacturing facilities are concerned.

Visitors such as Johann Georg Kohl and Robert Watt took umbrage at the industrial debris masking the falls' beauty. Limestone and wood filled the river and the base of the falls in 1860.

Early Settlements

AT THE FALLS

Fort Snelling

The first permanent white settlement near the falls was government supported to ensure the United States' hold on the territory ceded by the Dakota in 1805. Built at the junction of the Minnesota and Mississippi Rivers seven miles below the falls, Fort St. Anthony, later Fort Snelling, was an outpost in the wilderness.

~~~~~

Lieutenant Colonel Henry Leavenworth and his troops were dispatched to build the fort in 1819. He assessed the falls for their practical value and recommended that the war department build a sawmill and a gristmill there to supply the nearby fort with lumber and flour. Under his successor, **Colonel Josiah Snelling**, soldiers completed the mills and a barracks in 1823. In a letter to Thomas Jesup the next year, Colonel Snelling described these mills, the first to harness waterpower at the falls.

When in 1900 Sarah Thorp Heald painted an 1850s view of *Old Mill at St. Anthony Falls*, the falls had already powered saw and gristmills for nearly eight decades.

The Grist Mill is a fine building of stone, twenty five feet high from the bottom of the Cog-pit to the eaves; it is furnished with an excellent pair of burr stones and the flour manufactured the last year was equal to any in the world. The saw mill is a wooden frame building, in the ordinary form, the machinery is of the best kind, we have sawed in twenty four hours, three-thousand five hundred feet of pine plank; both of these mills are supplied with water from the falls, it is taken out at the table rock and conducted to the Mills by a race placed on the right bank of the river.

~~~~~

Arriving in Minnesota in 1820, **Philander Prescott** settled near Fort Snelling, where he worked as a fur trader and ran a store that supplied goods to the soldiers. His 1861 reminiscences describe construction logistics at the fort.

The saw mill was commenced in the fall and winter of 1820–21 and finished in 1822, and a large quantity of lumber was made for the whole fort, and all the furniture and outbuildings, and all the logs were brought to the mill or the landing by

*hand, and hauled from the landing to the mill, and from the mill to the fort by
teams. An officer by the name of Lieut. Croozer lived [with] and had charge of the
mill party. Supplies for the fort were all brought up in keel boats from St. Louis. It
generally took from fifty to sixty days to come from St. Louis to Fort Snelling. The
first steamboat that came to the Fort was a stern-wheeled boat from Cincinnati
with the contract for supplies for the troops in June, 1823.*

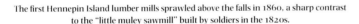

Colonel John H. Bliss set down his "Reminiscences of Fort Snelling" nearly sixty years
after his arrival there at age nine; his father, Major John Bliss, commanded the post from
1833 to 1837.

*The Falls of Saint Anthony, too, were picturesque; the government had a little
muley saw-mill there, and a small grist-mill, for grinding corn, all, of course, for
the use of the garrison; there, too, was kept our supply of beef cattle. All this neces-
sitated the erection of a comfortable building, for the sergeant and eight or ten men
who had charge of things, and this was all there then was of the splendid city of
Minneapolis. We used occasionally to have picnics there, and drove out a few times
of a winter night, had a hot supper and a whisky punch, and back to the Fort again,
with the coyotes howling about us, but rarely in sight. In no place I have ever seen
(and I have been in many) were the winter nights so clear and beautiful, and the
stars so many and so bright as there.*

The first Hennepin Island lumber mills sprawled above the falls in 1860, a sharp contrast
to the "little muley sawmill" built by soldiers in the 1820s.

The Founding of
St. Anthony

By treaty with the Dakota, the U.S. government owned the land along the Mississippi River from above St. Anthony Falls to its confluence with the Minnesota River. Joseph Plympton, Fort Snelling's commander in the 1830s, was only one of many who saw the value of the property bordering the falls. The owner of such property would also own the falls' waterpower by way of the traditional "riparian right" to the river's resources.

Plympton schemed to make this land privately available through "pre-emption rights." By declaring pre-emption, individuals who could show evidence of settlement—usually with a shanty cabin—could purchase the land from the government at a minimal price as soon as it became available. Plympton took measures to reestablish the boundary of the fort's military reservation *below* the eastern shore of the falls, altering the terms of the original treaty. But when word of the government's official redefinition of the boundaries arrived in 1838, Plympton was himself "pre-empted" by Fort Snelling's storekeeper, Franklin Steele, who benefited from political connections as the son of James Buchanan's campaign manager and as the brother-in-law of prominent fur-trader Henry Sibley, who would later be Minnesota's first governor. Steele built a shanty cabin overnight and beat out representatives sent by Plympton to stake his claim.

Franklin Steele fought off other claimants to become the first legal settler on the east side of the falls.

Having secured the east side of St. Anthony Falls, and well aware of the vast pinery stands along the Mississippi River to the north, Steele over the next decade built a dam and mill, both of which were completed in 1848. Lumberjacks cut the timber up north, floated the logs downriver to the St. Anthony millpond, and Steele's mill produced the boards that would build the town of St. Anthony, founded in 1849. By his own shrewd calculation, Steele had managed to insert himself on the bottom floor of the first industry at the falls. His St. Anthony Mill Company was the first of four early mills, and by 1856 the total sawing capacity on the falls' east side had risen to a hundred thousand board feet a day at high season, for an average annual yield of twelve million board feet. A great log harvest had begun, and it would feed the housing needs of the earliest settlers.

~~~~~~

John H. Stevens settled in Minnesota in 1849 and built the first house on the west bank land that would become Minneapolis. Stevens helped his friend Franklin Steele secure funding for his St. Anthony Mill Company. Widely respected on both sides of the river, Stevens recalled his pioneer days in an 1855 speech.

> *As we journeyed from the Fort the character of the country was beautiful beyond description. Not a solitary house except the old mill property was to be seen—an unbroken wilderness surrounded the site of Minneapolis. . . . The smoke of only two houses could be seen from St. Anthony. They stood there solitary and alone, money could hardly buy a meal, pork and beans and coffee was all that we expected if indeed we were thus favored. Little did I then think that St. Anthony would, in 1855, contain a population of near 3000, and Minneapolis 1000. . . . I determined to pitch my home on the west side of the Falls of St. Anthony, there to live, perhaps to die, and my present dwelling was erected in the winter of forty-nine and fifty, being the first house built in Minneapolis, by a private citizen.*

"For the first year our only neighbors were the Indians. We have often gone to bed at night, within our homestead, waked up in the morning and seen that while we were asleep the wigwams of either the Sioux, Chippewa or Winnebago had gone up," recalled John H. Stevens, whose house is barely visible at right in this 1854 daguerreotype.

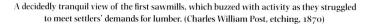

Daniel Stanchfield got his start as a lumberman in his home state of Maine. He settled in St. Anthony in 1847, logging on the Rum River and running a mercantile business in town. In 1853 he served as a representative to the territorial legislature. Stanchfield titled his 1899 recollections "History of Pioneer Lumbering on the Upper Mississippi and Its Tributaries."

Sumner W. Farnham ran the first sawmill during that autumn [1848], until he took charge of one of my logging parties in the winter. As soon as the mill started, it was run night and day in order to supply enough lumber for the houses of immigrants, who were pouring in from the whole country. There was life put into every enterprise. The houses had to be built of green lumber; and all merchandise came from St. Paul, or from the store of Franklin Steele at the fort. Dry lumber was hauled from Stillwater to finish the buildings. Both common and skilled laborers were scarce, as the mill company employed all they could possibly work on their improvements. Before Governor Ramsey proclaimed the organization of the Territory of Minnesota, June 1st, 1849, a busy town had grown up, called St. Anthony, built mostly by New England immigrants, and presenting the appearance of a thriving New England village.

When river navigation opened in 1849, on the first boats, immigration came in small armies. Every boat was full of passengers. The sawmills were all running to supply lumber to build houses for the newcomers, and this was continued through all the year, as long as navigation lasted. About half of the immigrants stopped at St. Paul. Both towns doubled in houses and families.

A decidedly tranquil view of the first sawmills, which buzzed with activity as they struggled to meet settlers' demands for lumber. (Charles William Post, etching, 1870)

An early arrival, **Rebecca Marshall Cathcart** moved with her mother and brothers to St. Anthony in 1849 and lived the rest of her life in the region. She recalled the early outpost in her 1915 "Sheaf of Remembrances."

The second day after our arrival a party was made up to visit St. Anthony Falls. . . . During our drive we saw several deer, and realized we were indeed in the wilderness. The thunder of the falling water reached our ears long before we came to the famous cataract; but when at last our eyes saw the great volume of water that rushed over the precipice, the sight surpassed all our expectations. It was superb; no one can realize now anything of the grandeur of the scene as it was then; no wonder that the poor Indian worshipped the Great Spirit of the cataract. But here again man has destroyed for utilitarian purposes what the savage worshipped.

Just five years after Rebecca Marshall Cathcart arrived to find only sawmills and one boarding house, St. Anthony was a bustling town, its main street often lined with Red River oxcarts.

The only building, except sawmills, at the Falls of St. Anthony at that time, May 11, 1849, was a boarding house for the mill hands. Two sawmills were operated on the east side just below Nicollet island; several small buildings were in the process of erection, however, and among them a one-story frame house was being built by my brothers, Joseph M. and William R. Marshall.

. . . People were pouring into the Territory; every steamboat's passenger list was full; every stage arriving in the village of St. Anthony was crowded with tourists; some came to settle, others to spy out the land. The stage stopped within a few rods of our house, and the tourists always crossed from our side of the river to Hennepin island, on a foot bridge, in order to get the best view of the Falls. They were invariably enraptured with the sight; as I have said, the fall of water at this time was grand, the river not being obstructed with logs, and the precipice over which the river dashed not having broken away.

Ann North moved to St. Anthony from New York with her husband John in 1849. During their six-year stay she wrote weekly to family members in the east; her parents received this early letter.

In the house we are coming on nicely. Have finally got a cupboard for dishes &c. It is a first-rate one—worth waiting for—Mr. North has made a cupboard for our clothes, so that we can keep them down here where they will be more dry than in the chamber. I never before knew any thing about living in houses made of lumber so green that water would drip from it. We, all, have to do so here—We have got the book case set up and filled—and it makes it seem quite like home. Yesterday, our mahogany furniture was all varnished, and it looks now about as nice as new. We got it done, with some fixing to the book case and painting and varnishing the cupboards, for $5 and we thought it quite worth it.

Ann North was just eighteen years old when she and her husband, John, moved halfway across the country from her parents.

Emily O. G. Grey joined her husband at St. Anthony in 1857. The daughter of a freed slave, she was an active member of Minneapolis's early black community, involved in various civic and religious organizations and causes. In recollections read to a group called the "Query Club" in 1893, she described female solidarity in the fledgling city of St. Anthony.

In the course of events, we all became established in our new homes. The lack of women's companionship began to be felt. The want was not long endured. First one neighbor called and then another, until we became acquainted and our visiting relations were easy and smooth. Fashionable and formal visits were not much in vogue, but the good, old-time neighborly calls . . . were more generally indulged in. A grateful remembrance of the kind deeds done for us by our new-made friends placed us in lifelong indebtedness. . . . [Friends gave me] suggestions in domestic economy. . . . New methods of breadmaking and vegetable cooking were learned. I was taught the art of baking that toothsome New England dish of "pork and beans" in the same way they were cooked in the lumber camps. This dish seemed to occupy the same relative degree of general enjoyment of a boiled dinner dish composed of sauerkraut, part of the pickled backbone of a pig, and Irish potatoes. There was always some woman friend who would gladly be to me a guiding star to lead me out of the many little difficulties met with in our households. . . .

~~~~~

Permelia A. Sanborn Atwater was the author of numerous pamphlets chronicling Minneapolis history. Married to Judge Isaac Atwater, who served on the Minnesota Supreme Court from 1858 to 1864, she published her reminiscences in 1894 under the title *Pioneer Life in Minneapolis: From a Woman's Standpoint, 1840–94.*

Both the spring of 1852 and '53 brought many emigrants to St. Anthony. The various professions and lines of business received solid accessions, besides many day laborers, that were much needed. There were no unoccupied dwellings, and many families were compelled to "camp out" until a house could be built. It was not always possible to do this at once, for the one saw mill could not turn out lumber rapidly enough to satisfy the demand. No reserve lumber could be accumulated, for every board, scantling and shingle was hauled away as soon as it came from the mill, and often, within twenty-four hours, formed part and parcel of a shelter and home for a newly arrived family.

In 1851, the *St. Anthony Express* called for tastefully built homes: "A well constructed house not only looks better but *is* better, and costs not more than an ill-contrived thing of the same size." The Roswell P. Russell house was built in 1847 from the first lumber sawed in St. Anthony. (B. F. Upton, photo)

We many times saw a load of lumber deposited on a lot in the evening, and by noon of the next day a balloon frame with board roof would appear in its stead, as if by magic—the familiar stove pipe sending up its wreaths of smoke, telling of the home and family life already established below. It must not be thought that these humble dwellings belonged only to the very poor. On the contrary they often sheltered well-to-do people, and those of the highest education and refinement. One often found in such tenements, boxes of books serving as tables and lounges, rolls of handsome carpets for seats and beds, fine paintings hanging on walls of rough pine boards, while crates of choice china and glass had to take their chances with the elements out of doors, till an addition could be made to the house. Not infrequently the carpets served as tapestry for the walls when an early winter caught the family in an unfinished house.

Suspension Bridge

I n 1854, the towns of Minneapolis and St. Anthony were physically linked by a suspension bridge that stretched from the western shore of the Mississippi River to Nicollet Island and then to the eastern shore. At a gala event on January 23, 1855, citizens celebrated this first-ever bridge over the full width of the Mississippi River. They marveled at the ease with which they could now cross the mighty river; no longer would they need to risk canoe passage or wait until winter to traverse by ice.

~~~~~

Jane Gay Fuller moved to St. Paul in 1854 and traveled widely throughout the state, collecting Indian legends and local lore that later appeared in her poems, short stories, and fiction. She described the inauguration of the suspension bridge in a letter to Hiram Fuller, her cousin and a newspaper editor who had the year before crossed the river by rope ferry, a journey he called "imminently perilous."

"From Our Correspondent of the Far West," published in the (New York) *Evening Mirror,* February 16, 1855.
There have been numerous festive gatherings of late, and the most interesting of all—the one still in the mouths of the multitude, was the opening of the Suspension Bridge—the first bridge (as every speaker on the occasion endeavored to impress upon the audience) which has ever spanned the old Father of Waters.

The event was celebrated on the 23rd, at St. Anthony. It was really a proud day for Minnesota, and one which will long be remembered by both citizens and strangers who were fortunate enough to be present. The morning was one of beautiful brightness. . . . The town was wide-awake on our arrival, and preparations making for the first grand, triumphal march of the East into the West. The procession was formed at the St. Charles, and consisted of a very long line of sleighs, (I dare not say how many as I did not count them, and the reports differ so much). One of mammoth size, with horses gaily decked, went forward with a band of music, and bearing aloft our national banner with its "Stripes and Stars," and then such music of sleigh-bells as followed, I am certain never before rose within the hearing of old St. Anthony.

It was with most singular sensations I looked out upon the scene, watching the procession as it passed on over Nicollet Island to the gates of the bridge, which sud-

*denly flew open, allowing it to pass on amid the cheers of the crowds, the thunder of
the cannon, the bugle-blasts of the band, and the sullen roar of the frozen cataract,—
under the evergreen arches, and over the first highway which has ever linked the
Eastern and Western valleys of the Mississippi.*

*The structure is a very fine one; strikingly harmonious in its proportions, and
corresponds beautifully with the character of the surrounding scenery. Literally, it
is a highway in the wilderness, over which Civilization, in her onward march, will
bear her lighted torches into the evening land of the West. Would like to furnish you
with a more scientific description of this superb fabric, but unfortunately have little
knowledge of mechanic laws. I only comprehended from the report, that the bridge
is 620 feet span; that it has a roadway of 17 feet, and that its cost was $36,000, the
entire contribution of stockholders who reside in St. Anthony and Minneapolis,
which last town has been built up almost entirely since you were here last June.*

The first suspension bridge across the Mississippi River provided the only link between Minneapolis and
St. Anthony until additional bridges were built after the two cities merged in 1872. Until 1870, the toll was
five cents for pedestrians and twenty-five cents for horse-drawn wagons. (Edwin D. Harvey, postcard)

From the *Minnesota Pioneer*, "Opening of the Wire Suspension Bridge Across the Mississippi," January 25, 1855.

It was a great day for Minnesota, and a signal and impressive mark of the spirit of progress which actuates her people, when on the Twenty-Third of January in the good year 1855, the citizens of Saint Anthony and Minneapolis in company with those of St. Paul and other places, inaugurated the completion of a bond by which the Father of Waters is, for the first time since its waters rolled from its source, in

The bridge tower offered "a view of the sparkling waters and the busy town" in 1868. By this time the towns were in fact busier than expected, and citizens were calling for a new, larger bridge to be built. (Beal's Gallery, photo)

Itasca lake, to the mighty Atlantic, spanned by as beautiful a structure as any that have been made in the United States, with all the aids that abundant capital could render. Since the days when Hernando de Soto first beheld its turbid waters, in the genial south, and Nicollet looked upon the Falls of Saint Anthony far in the North West, there has been no event so singular in its character, or so characteristic of an onward and practical spirit as that which was honored on Tuesday last; and the brightest feature which belongs to it, is that it is the result of individual enterprise, and the wise expenditure of local capital. No surer evidence of the solid progress of our Territory could be given than this which a portion of its citizens have rendered. Saint Anthony and Minneapolis have reason greatly to be proud of what has been accomplished, and the elegant structure which spans the "Father of Waters" will ever remain a monument of the liberality forecast and enterprise of their citizens.

From the *St. Anthony Express*, January 27, 1855.

Description of the Bridge

The towers on either side of the river are connected together by a sort of bridge work, which adds to their stability. The whole of this framing, which is of itself truly beautiful, is covered by a sheathing of boards; but much taste has been exhibited in this covering, to make amends for all the mechanical beauties that stand concealed within. The top of each tower is ornamented with a species of balcony over which a light roof is thrown, and their general appearance naturally suggests that they will be the resort of those who wish to enjoy, on a warm summer evening, as the sun sinks in the west, a view of the sparkling waters, and the busy towns on either side. . . . Blinds are placed in three sides of each tower, and add much to the appearance, though they are intended for ventilation. That portion of the frames connecting the towers is also covered in such a manner as to harmonize with the general character of the architecture. In each tower, there is an ornamental door, by which access may be had at any time to any portion of the frame, there being a stairway inside. There is also a neat window in each of the towers, which looks out on the river. This arrangement is also intended to accommodate the bridge keeper during the summer season. . . . Altogether the structure has a most fairy like appearance.

The Founding of Minneapolis

Unlike St. Anthony, the territory that became Minneapolis was securely located in the Fort Snelling military reservation. Squatters tried their luck with pre-emption rights on the west bank acreage, but many were expelled as the fort command arbitrarily granted settlement permits to some but not to others. Robert Smith, a congressman from Illinois, parlayed his political connections into a deal with the government that granted him the land on which the government gristmill stood. Franklin Steele schemed with John H. Stevens to claim land above the mill, and Stevens built the first house in what would become Minneapolis. Pressure to open the land to settlement resulted first in an 1852 law shrinking the military reservation's size, and next in an 1855 pre-emption clause rewarding the risk-takers who had already built on military property. By the time settlement was legally permitted on the west side, St. Anthony's sawmills had allowed that community to surge ahead of the fledgling enterprises of Minneapolis. Later, however, the two communities would view themselves as a united manufacturing center competing against their downriver rival, St. Paul.

Minneapolis's first mayor, Dorilus Morrison, like many of the area's early entrepreneurs, pursued diverse interests at the falls.

Dorilus Morrison was a pioneering Minneapolis businessman whose vast interests included lumber, waterpower, railroads, flour, cotton, and machinery manufacturing. A Maineite who in 1854 came to Minnesota in search of pinelands, Morrison soon began operating a sawmill in St. Anthony. He was one member of the twelve-man partnership that became the powerful Minneapolis Milling Company, which regulated industries at the west side falls and nearby lands. He built and ran the Excelsior Mill, incorporated the Minneapolis Cotton Manufacturing Company and the Minneapolis Flour Manufacturing Company, and oversaw the construction of the Northern Pacific Railway.

In addition to his lucrative pioneer sawmill, Franklin Steele also controlled the ferry across the Mississippi River at Fort Snelling, pictured here in 1861. His friend John H. Stevens managed a similar rope ferry at the falls, maintaining the transportation lines between St. Anthony and Minneapolis. (Joel E. Whitney, photo)

∼∼∼∼∼

Just as some had lamented the European name given to the falls, others argued against an anglicized moniker for the city growing up on its west side. While some suggested the name Lowell, in honor of Massachusetts's water-powered industrial city, others considered West St. Anthony or All Saints. In 1852, amid much debate, newcomer **Charles Hoag** suggested a semi-indigenous name, and it gradually gained favor among the inhabitants of the west side.

From the *St. Anthony Express*, November 5, 1852.

Minnehapolis, opposite St. Anthony,

November 5, 1852

We are accustomed, on this side of the river, to regard your paper as a sort of exponent of public sentiment, & as a proper medium of public expression.

My purpose, in this communication, is to suggest a remedy for the anomalous position we occupy of dwelling in the place selected by the constituted authorities of Hennepin county as the county seat; which as yet bears no [name], unless the

> *miserable misnomer, All Saints, shall be considered so thrust upon us that the unanimous determination of the inhabitants cannot throw it off. It is a name that is applicable to no more than two persons in the vicinity of the falls, and of doubtful application even to them.*
>
> *The name I propose [is] Minnehapolis, derived from* Minne ha-ha *laughing water, with the Greek affix* polis, *a city, meaning "Laughing water City," or "city of the Falls." You perceive I spell it with an* h *which is silent in the pronunciation.*
>
> *This name has been very favorably received by many of the inhabitants to whom it has been proposed, and unless a better can be suggested it is hoped that this effort to christen our place will not prove as abortive as those heretofore named. I am aware that other names have been proposed such as Lowell, Brooklyn, Addiesville &c., but until some one is decided upon we intend to call ourselves Minnehapolis.*

The *St. Anthony Express* editorial response appeared a week later, on November 12.

> *Minnehapolis—When the communication proposing this name for the promising town growing up on the other side of the river was last week handed to us we were so much engaged as to have no time to comment. The name is an excellent one, and deserves much favor from the citizens of the capital of Hennepin. No other in our opinion could be chosen that would embody to the same extent the qualities desirable in a name. The* h *being silent, as our correspondent recommends, and as custom would soon make it, it is poetical and euphonious; the nice adjustment of the Indian* minne, *with the Greek* polis, *forms a beautiful compound, and, finally, it is as all names should be when it is possible, admirably descriptive of the locality. By all means, we would say, adopt this beautiful and exceedingly appropriate title, and do not longer suffer abroad from connection with the meaningless and outlandish name of "All Saints."*

~~~~~

With town names firmly established and population growing by leaps and bounds, Minneapolis and St. Anthony became home to settlers who recorded not only their hardships but also their occasions for optimism and joy.

An 1856 newcomer from New York, **Harlow A. Gale** pursued a career in real estate in Minneapolis. After his death, his family collected his papers and published *Minneapolis: A Short Reversal of Human Thought. Being the Letters and Diary of Mr. Harlow A. Gale, 1857 to 1859.*

> *June 6 [1857]. I believe I was talking of Minneapolis. I think the number of buildings has doubled since March. They average more than one a day. 'Tis exciting,*

I assure you. I don't know as you care about all this but it will help you to form some opinion of where I live. There are two Hotels going up, one 100 by 120 feet; the other, 100 by 166; three churches; school-houses and dwellings daily and nightly. Oh, we have a beautiful town! You may judge further of our attractions when I tell you that my brothers, Amory and S. C., are here, and today S. C. sent for his books and clothes. This will surprise Millbury friends, who think I am among Indians and wolves and a fit residence only for either a culprit or cannibal.

June 30. The sun has at length gone down to the great relief of citizens of the town, for it has been unusually warm today,—100 in the shade at noon. The people are luxuriating in the refreshing cool of early eve, sitting in doorways, strolling in the street, and drinking soda water. We would either walk down on Suspension Bridge that I have spoken of so often to you, and that I love so much at this hour, or we'd ride down the Prairie so fresh with the odors of flowers and grains.

Until the 1860s, St. Anthony and Minneapolis were tourist towns. St. Anthony's imposing Winslow House hotel was built to accommodate visitors to the falls, and B. F. Upton captured this panorama of St. Anthony's main street, Hennepin Island, and Minneapolis from the hotel in 1857. At the left are the platform sawmills that, along with other industries, gradually conquered the river and reduced its visual appeal.

Edwin Clark moved from New Hampshire to Minnesota in 1857 and on September 28 of that year began publishing the first daily newspaper in St. Anthony–Minneapolis, the *Falls Evening News*. He later served as Indian agent for the Ojibwe near Crow Wing and still later followed yet another career path when he returned to Minneapolis as an insurance agent. He described an early Fourth of July celebration in his autobiography.

Arrangements for an extensive patriotic celebration on Monday, July 5th. . . . It was voted to have a barbecue, a general free picnic, speeches, music, dancing, etc. on Nicollet Island . . . the citizens of St. Anthony were to meet at the Winslow House square at eleven A.M., and the citizens of Minneapolis in the park in front of the Nicollet House at the same time, and at the signal of three guns, at twelve o'clock, the processions were to commence moving to Nicollet Island, and at the same time the six church bells were to be rung and the second National Salute of thirty-two guns fired for the thirty-two States of the Union, of which Minnesota, the youngest would be only forty-two days old. . . . The day was a splendid one for such a Holiday and was appreciated by the ten to twelve thousand people present on the festive occasion. There were several banners suspended; near the entrance to the grounds was one reading "St. Anthony (clasped hands) Minneapolis" symbolizing a desirable union which was not accomplished until fourteen years later.

In an 1870 view from the Winslow House hotel, Minneapolis outpaces neighboring St. Anthony in population and industry. St. Anthony officially became part of the city of Minneapolis in 1872. (William W. Wales, photo)

∼∼∼∼∼

Lawyer **Charles Henry Woods** settled in Minneapolis in 1866 and served as the city's first justice the next year. An early letter to his friend Gilman Henry Tucker depicts a booming local economy.

After two weeks stay in this rapidly growing town, I will give you some of my impressions in regard to it. Its situation I suppose you already know to be on the westerly side of St. Anthony's Falls 10 miles above St. Paul. The population of this place and St. Anthony—which are practically one, being connected by a Suspension Bridge over the Mississippi—is at present about 11,000.

The town presents a most decidedly unfinished appearance in consequence of the buildings and other improvements now in progress. It is a common remark that not less than 1,000 buildings will be erected here the present season. My own impression, however, is that to reach that number it would be necessary to take into the account an occasional barn and possibly two or three of those edifices that are usually about four feet square.

I suppose if one were to reckon such buildings only as might fairly be reckoned in describing the increase . . . (such as dwellings, mills & business blocks), he could doubtless number six or seven hundred. At all events, the town is advancing as fast as capital enterprise & industry can push it. Most of the new blocks are of stone and will compare favorably with similar buildings in eastern cities.

I cannot think it is a matter of speculation to say that this is bound to become a business point of the first importance in the Northwest. There are solid reasons for such a statement which need only to be mentioned to be appreciated: 1. It is the head of navigation on the Mississippi River. 2. There is the greatest water power here which is perfectly available for manufacturing purposes to be found in the United States. 3. The country about here, as a grain growing region, is unsurpassed in the West. 4. The climate is one supremely healthy. These are the natural advantages.

Again the tide of emigration is rapidly setting in this direction. The country is rapidly filling up. New railroads are in process of construction and new towns [are] springing into existence in all directions. Natural causes alone, I apprehend, are sufficient to make this a central point. Lumber mills & flour mills are doing an enormous business this season.

TEXTILE MILLS

With its waterpower potential, Minneapolis had long been compared to Lowell, Massachusetts, and from its earliest days entrepreneurs dreamed of developing a similar textile industry there. The mills of St. Anthony Falls were a natural destination, via the Mississippi River, for southern-grown cotton. Still, it was not until 1870 that the first such enterprise was incorporated: the Minneapolis Cotton Manufacturing Company, headed by Dorilus Morrison. In a decade of operation, its factory produced bags, wagon covers, and awnings. The bags fed other local industry, as they replaced the barrels in which flour had customarily been packed.

Despite these local interconnections, cotton milling did not catch on as many had expected, most likely because of Minneapolis's distance from eastern markets and shipping centers. Similarly, woolen mills proved largely unsuccessful, with one notable exception. The North Star Woolen Mill opened in 1864 under W. W. Eastman and Paris Gibson, and when they declared bankruptcy in 1876, the Minneapolis Mill Company bought the facility, thereby saving the business and its numerous jobs. The mill manufactured scarves, flannels, blankets, and yarns and survived as a significant industry in Minneapolis until the 1940s.

Blankets are displayed in the North Star Woolen Mills showroom in 1910. One steady customer was Chicago's Pullman Palace Car Company, which used the blankets in both America and Europe.

From the *St. Paul Pioneer Press*, July 12, 1865.

Woollen Factories: Making Cloth

The manufacturing process is highly interesting. The wool is first assorted and classified into five or six grades, from whence it goes to the washer, where it is washed, passed through two large vats by steam, and thoroughly cleaned. It is then placed in a large, steam tub and rapidly dried, after which it passes to the pick-ing room, and is picked to pieces by machinery, the services of a man only being required to feed the machine. From the picking room it goes to the carding machine, to the spinners, and lastly to the looms of the weavers. . . .

This mill is now manufacturing cassimeres, jeans, santinets, plain plaids, fancy goods, and will soon commence the manufacture of blankets. They are now experimenting with some new colors and in a short time expect to be able to furnish first class magentas, &c. They are just commencing to manufacture fancy flannels.

North Star Woolen Mill workers sort fleece into various grades. Sixty years after the *Pioneer Press* described the process, the first step remained unchanged. (J. H. Kammerdiener, photo)

From the *Minneapolis Tribune,* January 12, 1877.

The tribune takes pleasure in announcing this morning the consummation of an arrangement of more consequence to Minneapolis than the result of half-a-dozen presidential elections: the purchase by the Minneapolis Mill Company, of which C. C. Washburn, Dorilus Morrison, W. D. Washburn, and R. J. Baldwin are the proprietors, of the North Star Woolen Mills . . .

The importance to Minneapolis of the consummation of this arrangement can hardly be overestimated. The mills, in which our citizens have for so many years taken so great an interest, and in whose superior products they have indulged a pardonable pride, have been rescued from their misfortunes, and put upon a basis of strength and efficiency which they have never before enjoyed.

. . . They have done it with no purposes of speculation or expectation of profit; but with a view solely to the welfare of the city, and with the end of diversifying as much as possible the manufacturing industries conducted at the falls. They desire, also, that the well-earned reputation of the North Star Woolen Mills (which took the premium for the finest blankets in the world,) shall be maintained, and that Minneapolis shall continue to be known as the headquarters of this maufacture.

Eva Gay was the pseudonym of Eva McDonald Valesh, who moved to Minnesota with her parents and siblings in 1877. Trained as a typesetter, proofreader, and teacher, she found her public calling when the  *St. Paul Globe* editor sought a reporter to explore the lives of working women in the Twin Cities. Valesh researched her stories undercover, applying for jobs and interviewing women who labored in factories and as servants. The series was published for nearly a year, after which Valesh wrote a labor column for the paper. She later moved east, where she was active in politics as a writer and editor.

From the St. Paul Globe, May 20, 1888.

Workers in Wool

I saw clearly that I was not going about the right way to find the real condition of the girls. So next morning I carefully fished out of the rag-bag a rather dilapidated dress, having borrowed a hat and jacket to match, tied my hair in a careless knot, and procured shoes and gloves with many holes in them. When my disguise was completed, I looked as if I hadn't eaten a square meal in a long time. Hoping that my wretched appearance would provoke pity, I presented myself at the office of the mill and asked for work. . . .

I noticed that the mill was extremely clean, the walls and ceilings were white-washed, and even the floors looked as if they had often been scrubbed.

"You have a clean place to work in, at any rate," I remarked to one girl.

"Yes, its clean up here," she said, "but if you want to see the hardest looking work room in the city just go down in the basement in the old part of the mill."

"What's down there?"

"That's the room where the blankets and flannels are washed and dried," she said. "I've worked here for years and I never go down there except to wash an apron. You just go down and stay a few minutes and see if you won't be glad to get out of there."

I went down to the room mentioned. There were a number of men at the machines; at first I could see no girls. This room is lighted by windows partly below the level of the sidewalk, which makes the light rather dim. The heat from the washing and drying machines was so intense (98 deg.) that I was on the point of leaving, but just then spying some girls over near the windows, I thought if they could work in that place day after day, surely I could stand it for a half an hour. The floor was dirty and little streams of soap suds ran from the washing machines. Picking my way across the damp floor I found some girls working on heavy machines called "gigs;" others were "bushing," or picking specks off the blankets when finished.

"Girls, why don't you open the windows, it's so hot here?" I exclaimed.

"None of your business" was the prompt reply. "If you don't like this place keep away."

I assured them that I meant no offense, but was looking for work my self.

They explained that the girls in the other departments looked down on them for working in such a dirty place.

"But why don't you open the windows?" I persisted.

"We get used to the heat, so we don't mind it much, and we can stand that better than the dust and dirt from the street above," they said.

"How much are you paid?"

"Ninety cents a day."

"Do you think it's worth while to ruin your health by working in this place for such wages?"

"I don't know as it is," was the weary reply; "but when a girl's got her living to earn she can't choose where she'll work." . . .

In the basement of the new addition were the girls who finished and pressed the blankets. This was the most pleasant department of the mill. It was well lighted, clean and cool, and the work was arranged so that the girls could sit if they chose. It was a sharp contrast to the wash and dry room in the other basement near by.

I found the average wages in all departments, except weaving, to be 90 cents a day. In some places the work was light and tolerably clean, but the girls complained that, with few exceptions, they had to stand at their work all day, and of course were very tired at night.

The weavers received the highest wages, earning from $1 to $1.35 a day, and occasionally a fast worker could earn $2 a day on good material.

The weaving is such hard work that many complain that although their wages seem good, yet they cannot work all the year around, often having to stay and rest, or perhaps pay a large doctor's bill out of their earnings.

"How long can a girl work steady without injuring her health?" I asked.

Of course there were various opinions: foreigners would last longer than Americans, but the general opinion was that three or four years of steady work were sufficient to finish a girl's usefulness.

"Where do they go then?"

"Some get married; some go to the hospital, and we don't know anything about many of them; they just drop out and others take their places," was the answer.

Many of the girls were stoop-shouldered and thin, but others were as bright and handsome girls as one could find in higher walks of life.

"The superior machinery of this mill enables the proprietors to turn out a most acceptable cloth, specially adapted to our climate, and being made from the superior wool of the State, is most durable in wear and beautiful in texture and finish," observed the *Minneapolis Tribune*. Forty years later, in 1905, workers at North Star Woolen Mills were still maintaining those standards.

PAIL, TUB, & LUMBER MANU. FACTORY.
PLANING. MATCHING, PLITTING.

Lumbering

AT THE FALLS

The Sawmill Towns

The first industry around which St. Anthony and Minneapolis were built was saw milling. In 1856, the annual output was about twelve million board feet. By 1869, it had risen almost sevenfold to 90,734,595, and by 1899 another tenfold to 960,000,000. The sawmills were at first evenly divided between the two cities, with six on the east side and seven on the west, but between 1858 and 1869 eight more mills rose on the west side near the dam.

Life in the city followed the sawmills' seasonal cycle. In autumn, crews left for the northern pineries, and the slower current of the Mississippi River stilled the saws. When the waters rose again in the spring, logs from the north floated into the millponds, backing up and filling the river for miles. The mills drew logs from the millponds, sawed them, and deposited the boards on an adjoining platform for use by local individuals and industries, or for shipment to points east and south. Numerous related industries sprang up, including planing mills to smooth the lumber; sash, door, and blind factories; manufacturers of shingles and wooden buckets; and fuel companies that advertised the use of sawdust to heat homes.

The falls' first important industry—sawmilling—was launched in the 1850s. Steam-powered mills like the Nelson-Tenny, painted by Ferdinand Uebel in 1901, dominated the trade after 1880, when many mills, no longer dependent on waterpower, relocated above Hennepin Avenue.

Twenty-four-year-old **Francis Wilkinson** ventured to the United States from England in 1855. He sojourned in Boston, Chicago, Minneapolis, St. Louis, and Kansas City—seeking his fortune and "the romantic life"—before returning to England in the late 1860s. His travelogue, "Here and There in America," was published in the *West Yorkshire Pioneer* in 1869.

St. Anthony I found to be a small settlement containing about 1,000 inhabitants. It is on the left or east bank of the Mississippi, in the state of Minnesota (an Indian name signifying water-country, this state abounding in lakes, many of which are very extensive and of surpassing beauty). The chief employment of the settlers was that of "lumbering," or "logging," a hard enough life, certainly, but by [no] means devoid of interest or excitement. These lumberers usually

Logging was a winter activity because lumberjacks moved the large logs with sleds and skids. (Whitney and Zimmerman, postcard)

start off in groups and proceed up the river; after travelling a considerable distance, they then strike off into the immense pine forests and begin their arduous task of cutting down the pine, and other trees. When the trees are felled and all their branches lopped off, they are cut into logs of convenient sizes for being dragged to the river, to which they are taken and placed upon the ice. There these logs remain until the ice breaks up; when away they go rolling, ducking, and tumbling one over the other, down the river, looking more like porpoises at play than inanimate blocks of wood. This expeditious and cheap mode of transit is much valued by the settlers, as, of course, all their logs are delivered "carriage paid." In case of injury or loss, however, there is the disadvantage of having no one to fall back upon for "damages." The logs are brought up at some convenient trading point, and a general re-assortment takes place; every "lumberer" having placed a distinctive mark on his logs, identification is a comparatively easy task.

From the *St. Anthony Express*, June 3, 1854.

The Falls

As you stand on the West bank of the river, opposite the cataract, during the present stage of high water, a most beautiful and imposing sight is presented. The dark and turbid river, swollen by the recent rains, pours an immense column of water over the precipice. The huge jam of logs, piled high on the brink of the Falls, divides the stream into different volumes. The width of the fall on the west side, from the bank to the first jam is perhaps a hundred feet. Here the current is deepest and the descent most perpendicular. The waters seem scarcely broken, or changed in color till they reach the abyss below,—a broad basin formed by the surrounding rocks and heaped up logs, of snow white, foaming, angry waters, whirling and boiling, in ceaseless eddies, impatient of restraint. Into this deep chasm, plunge the hurrying waters, with continuous, sullen roar, and escaping from their brief confinement, flow swiftly onward, in a wide track of white foam, as they dash against the huge rocks which obstruct their progress.

But at this season, in addition to the greatly increased volume of water which flows over them, a new feature of interest enhances the beauty of the Falls. Through this narrow gate way of a hundred feet in width, the great pine forests of the north seek an outlet to the market in the far south. The huge logs come floating on, singly

At the rim of "the boiling cauldron," the brave subject of this 1855 photograph is dwarfed by the massive logs stalled there.

or in squads, and are hurled length-wise into the deep abyss, sometimes striking the concealed rocks with a force which causes the adjoining bank where you stand to tremble beneath your feet. They disappear for a time after their plunge, again to emerge at a distance from the point where they struck, but still within the seething "dell of waters," raging in the basin formed by the cataract. Now you get an idea of the tremendous force of the element before you. These mighty monarchs of the forest, some of them three and four feet in diameter, are caught up by the whirling eddies, and hurled ten feet heavenward, with the same ease that you would toss a shingle in the air. They fall back into the boiling cauldron, pitching, diving, bounding, bruising, grinding among each other and the rocks, until some chance stroke drives them over the edge of the basin, and they float away to lodge again perchance, on the great pile stretching away on the shallow rapids for a long distance below, or perchance to find their way into the St. Paul boom. So the process continues day by day, until the whole winter's work of our hardy lumbermen, has passed the dangerous 'chute' and found its destined market.

Isaac Metcalf, a visitor from Maine, wrote to his wife on July 12, 1855, while a guest at St. Paul's Winslow House hotel.

The fall is now about half covered with Jams of Pine Logs. Right under the Main Fall on the Minneapolis side, the presumptuous Yankees have stuck in a Saw Mill, which is cutting away finely. . . . Minneapolis and St. Anthony are connected above the Falls by a fine Wire Suspension Bridge—like the one at Niagara. St. Anthony is a great focus of the Lumber business, and is most all Maine Men. About at the head—that is about the largest operator is one Sam'l Stanchfield formerly of Milo, Piscatagnis Co. Me. He has a large store at St. Anthony, Mills, Lumber Yards & Lumbering at various places. His profits this year are extimated at not less than $10,000 clear!

John McCoy, a visitor to St. Anthony Falls in 1857, recorded his impressions of the lumber trade there.

I visited here some of the large plank factorys, where I beheld the great logs in one department, saw it there whirled into plank, cast off into another, and another until it came out finely plained, polished and ready in every way for use. The length of

*time consumed in sawing through a large log was just one quarter of a minute by
the watch. The saws are all circular. Then too by the same machinery shingles are
made of the best quality. The wood used for the engine is also sawed by the same machinery, clipping it in two as shears clipping bits of paper. . . .*

*Minneapolis and St Anthony are to be the center of the lumber trade in the
State. The amount of lumber in the log brought out of Rum river and its tributaries, last spring, was 150,000,000 feet, which was worth on this market (in the log)
from $6.50 to $7.50 per thousand, amounting in the aggregate to not less than
$1,050,000.00. The majority of these logs were floated over the Falls, rafted and
conveyed to the southern markets, instead of being manufactured into lumber, as
will eventually be the case at this point.*

∽∽∽∽∽

"Viator" was the pseudonym of a Pennsylvanian who chronicled his 1857 Minnesota
travels in numerous letters to his hometown newspaper editor.

August 19, 1857

*A tremendous water power is created at these falls. All the machinery of the
world almost must be driven in the space of this mile of dashing water. An immense
amount of pine lumber is sawed here. The logs are driven down from the pinery up*

Timber clogging the rapids in 1860. The logs likely escaped the sawmills' reach by tumbling over the falls, where they damaged the limestone ledge and continued the erosion of the falls. (Edwin D. Harvey, postcard)

By 1860 several sawmills already filled a platform erected over the river; more would follow.

at the head waters, manufactured into lumber and rafted to the country below. There are two bridges across the river at this point—one a wire suspension, the other a wooden structure.

There is something grand and striking in these falls of St. Anthony. But man has marred God's beautiful workmanship. His sacrilegious hands are laid upon this mighty cataract that for many centuries had been sounding the awful Diapason of the Creator's praise. The roar of the waters is now mingled with the hum of machinery. The breast of the fall is laden with sawlogs and the entire region cumbered with lumber. This utility of ours—it is the ruin of the beautiful—the harmonious—the poetic. Man in his grasping after the coin of earthly stamp would mar the stamp of heaven.

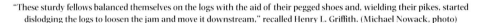

While the loggers and the sawyers may not have found much time to write about this hectic boom period, many young boys would fondly recall their days growing up in the "sawmill towns" of St. Anthony and Minneapolis.

Henry L. Griffith worked in the wholesale food business as an adult, but, as he recalled in *Minneapolis: The New Sawdust Town,* his youth was steeped in the lumber trade on the city's north side.

> *My best playgrounds were the big lumberyards near the mills. One of these yards, where "green" lumber was stored for months before being placed on the market, was located only a block from our Fifth Street home.*
>
> *All the neighborhood boys used this lumber yard as play space, and the mill owners, far from objecting to our trespass, silently approved. They knew that boys were alert and observant, and would quickly note any pilfering of their property. Our games were exciting, and as I look back on them, rather dangerous. We jumped from pile to pile, and the piles were some 30 feet high.*
>
> *The lumber was stacked so that the ends of boards, at intervals, extended about two feet from the pile. These made high steps by which we could mount to the top in no time. The ground of the yard had a thick covering of sawdust, spread there so that the horse-drawn lumber wagons would not sink in the mud in wet weather. We exercised ourselves in a wide repertoire of lumber yard games. . . .*

"These sturdy fellows balanced themselves on the logs with the aid of their pegged shoes and, wielding their pikes, started dislodging the logs to loosen the jam and move it downstream," recalled Henry L. Griffith. (Michael Nowack, photo)

I often visited the sawmills, which lined the river all the way from Hennepin Avenue northward to Camden Place. What interested me most was the way the great logs were pulled out of the river by chain runways and then cut into lumber lengths by the huge whining saws. . . .

The sawmills' big year was 1899. This was when I was 17 years old. But on many a year before this, when the spring thaws came, my mother used to load us into her one-horse buggy, tuck us under bearskin robes and take us to see the log jam up river. We drove along the banks of the Mississippi until we reached a vantage point a little above Camden Place.

Here we drew up to watch the log jam, a great spectacle which I enjoyed as much as a circus. The logs, no longer floating calmly down the current, seemed to have fought furiously with one another as if each were trying to get downstream first. They were jammed and pushed up at every possible angle in a tight-packed topsy-turvy jumble.

Logjams might cause the river to back up for miles, overflow its banks, and destroy structures on shore. As more and more logs were added to the jam, the task of untangling them became increasingly complicated, not to mention dangerous. (B. F. Upton, postcard, ca. 1865)

Later, when all the river ice had melted, Mother would give us another grand treat by driving us to the lower end of the jam to watch the lumberjacks. . . . I never tired of watching the log-rolling contest held on the river. This was certainly no game for amateurs. The log rollers had plenty of practice behind them in their daily work, and they were practically unbeatable.

∼∼∼∼∼

Melvin L. Frank was born in Hudson, Wisconsin, and grew up in north Minneapolis. An ordained minister of the United Church of Christ, he served Midwestern congregations for more than fifty years. He recalled his childhood in Minneapolis (1910–1920) in an unpublished memoir, "Sawmill City Boyhood."

For us boys the sawmill always offered the number one attraction in summertime outdoor activity. A lot of it was against the lumberyard rules; that only added zest to our adventures. . . .

It was great to spend time riding the narrow gauge trucks and playing in the shavings house, but that was not nearly as fascinating as the big sawmill itself

At the C. A. Smith mill in Minneapolis in 1885 logs are pulled up from the river, "scoured" with a blast of water to remove dirt, then swallowed by the mill, later to emerge as boards, shingles, and sawdust. (Underwood and Underwood, photo)

where occasionally we could venture onto the long catwalk that overlooked the whining, thrumming scene where logs were cut up into lumber. As long as we stayed on the walk-way and out of danger we were permitted to watch the operation.

Most enthralling, I guess, was the start of the wet log on the way to becoming lumber. It came, dripping, up from the river on an endless chain-lift runway to where it was maneuvered onto the carriage by the chief sawyer who supervised every cut of the log. He was the most important man in the process, because it was his know-how that produced the highest yield possible from every log.

When it was "dogged" to the carriage this steam powered machine drove the log into the whirring band saw that made the initial cut, and then with lightning speed reversed its motion back to the starting position, flipped the log and fastened it in place and rode it to the next cut. We kids wondered how the setter on the carriage kept from getting thrown from his place on the shot-gun return after each cut. Equally amazing was the way in which the steam operated clamps turned the log and held it in place while it was being sawed.

As we continued on the catwalk we saw the boards move from the saw on steam powered rollers to the next saws that trimmed them to the desired width and cut them into standard lengths. Moving continuously and given only an occasional assist by a mill hand, the lumber was processed until it emerged from the huge factory shed, stacked in neat piles and loaded on the narrow gauge trucks for removal by a yard man driving his horse and taking it to its assigned place for seasoning. We kids knew how the men piled the lumber, reversing each course so the pile could breathe and the boards dry out evenly.

One of the Sixth Street dads, Cliff Borgen's father, worked in the saws shop handling the big saws that required regular sharpening. Both band saws and circular saws of various sizes were used in the mill. When they came into the shop the men would mount them on stands where they could be worked on with grinding wheels and hand files which were used in the sharpening process. Those saws seemed to sing as they vibrated in response to the file or wheel. Sparks flew. They had to be watched lest a fire start. Working in the big mill was exciting. We boys could see that.

Throughout the sawmill leather belts drove the machinery. Overhead spinning shafts were suspended from building beams and power take-offs transferred power to the belts. Everywhere belts flapped as they moved from pulley to pulley. Such a mixture of sounds a sawmill made.

~~~~~~

Paul Gyllstrom was an editor and columnist for the *Minneapolis Times* from 1904–1905. In his "Notes on Early Minneapolis," written in the 1920s, he recalled his youthful adventures in the 1870s.

The log driving season offered great sport. In those days the saw mills were only a short distance above the St. Anthony Falls. The loggers working at the booms had

Bustling with loaders, stackers, sellers, and buyers, the J. Dean & Co. lumberyard in 1874 was an enticing playground for neighborhood children.

instructions to let logs with certain markings pass through for the mills at St. Paul. Logs of all sizes, up to two feet and a half in diameter, would come slushing along, and the larger they were the better they suited our purpose. It was a wonderful sight as one thinks of it now to see those "river rats"—not one of whom could have been more than ten years old—executing some fanciful dive, climbing back, and setting themselves for another plunge.

Walter Ernest Dexter spent his childhood not in play but in work at the lumberyards.

When we came here there was five sawmills on the falls there in Minneapolis on the west side of the Mississippi and then there were five on the east side of the river. . . . We got there in 1885, and I went to work with father in '86 in the Shevlin mill. I pulled laths in the lath mill the first season that I worked in the mill . . .

We lived, well, I would say that it was pretty nearly two miles from the mill on the east side in St. Anthony. And, of course, I walked both ways. Father used the streetcar. I didn't make enough to spend money for carfare in those days. It was customary to get up shortly after five o'clock for me. That made quite a day for my mother. The mill was ten miles from the house. . . . My lunch would be two sandwiches, a piece of pie, a cookie or a doughnut, and let's see, I drank water. We didn't drink either tea or coffee then, the young folks. I drank water at the mill. We ate lunch at twelve o'clock—twelve to one.

Sawmill workers pause from cutting logs and loading lumber, ca. 1900. (Scholl, photo)

River rats and lumberyard gamesters: children pose in 1890 on the bank of the Mississippi River at Bohemian Flats, where log and lumber salvaging was integral to the local economy.

. . . The mills operated only during the summer months in Minneapolis and when they shut down, generally around the first of November, we had to hop out and find something else to do. Well, there was generally a job in a box factory or a planing mill or a sash and door shop or the molding room of the sash and door shop or the rip-saw or the cut-off saw. Also, if it was really bad, real hard like during the Cleveland panic—in '92–'96—I would hop out on the ice fields and get about six or eight weeks cutting ice. But the boys nowadays don't realize what we used to get for wages, but we had to be on the ice field as soon as we could see and we couldn't leave as long as we could see, and we got a dollar and ten cents a day. I put in three or four different winters doing that.

Saw milling at St. Anthony Falls was phased out in the 1870s and 1880s. The Minneapolis Mill Company, concerned about damages to the limestone ledge caused by logs that escaped the booms, bought up the mills it had been renting and gradually silenced their saws. The development of steam engines also reduced millers' dependence on waterpower, and many moved their operations to north Minneapolis, which offered more space and easy access both to the river and to railroads. There, between 1899 and 1905, the mills turned out enough lumber to guarantee Minneapolis's title as the nation's leading sawmill center—temporarily. By 1921 the northern pineries were exhausted and the industry rapidly declined.

THE GATEWAY DISTRICT

Situated on the river and on major rail lines, Minneapolis was hailed as "the Gateway to the Northwest," welcoming immigrants, settlers, and visitors alike. The city's own Gateway was located in the triangle formed by Hennepin, Nicollet, and Washington Avenues, just west of the mill district. The original heart of the city, this area offered amusements, banks, retail stores, and restaurants to the local population by 1867. The Gateway Building housed a bureau of information for the thousands of people who stepped off the trains at the Union Depot looking for work. From this point, many found positions in local industries or set off for the northern pineries or western farm fields.

This area was also a popular stopping point for seasonal laborers out of work and eager to spend their recent earnings: lumberjacks spent their summers in the Gateway while migrant farm hands sought shelter during Minnesota winters. By the early 1900s, banks and merchants were leaving the district, to be replaced by saloons, cheap lodgings, and pawnshops. Although efforts were made to revitalize this area—a city park complete with ornate fountain and pavilion was constructed from 1908–1915 and the Union City Mission began serving the transient population in the 1910s—by 1917 the Gateway district had been condemned as a skid row. Adding to its reputation, the Industrial Workers of the World (IWW), finding many sympathizers in the district's migrant workers, organized there and sent representatives to Minnesota's wheat fields and lumber camps to encourage workers to rise up against the ruling class and its wage system.

Long viewed as an area in need of redevelopment because of its crowded population and deteriorated housing, the Gateway district was the target of urban renewal in the 1950s and 1960s, when buildings were torn down and rebuilt and the population—many of them elderly, foreign-born males, former lumberjacks and railroad employees—relocated to Nicollet Island, Cedar-Riverside, and other housing developments.

The result of an early wave of city improvements, Gateway Park offered a green haven and a refreshing fountain as well as information for tourists and recent arrivals. (Charles P. Gibson, photo)

An idyllic Gateway Park in this 1920 postcard is bounded by the Union City Mission, which served a population of transients and operated the St. James Hotel, which offered sleeping accommodations for up to 600 men.

ARTIFICIAL LIMBS

A vast amount of heavy machinery was driven by the falls, and the belts, pulleys, saws, and large gears that hummed in the lumber and flour mills were both difficult to start and difficult to stop. Such machinery could lead to disastrous accidents, and in response to the needs of workers in the mills, on the farms, and on the railroads, Minneapolis became a major center for the design and manufacture of prostheses, a reputation it retains today.

From the *American Miller*, April 1881.

On March 4 . . . millwright James Donelson . . . caught his coat in the gear of the chop conveyor in the basement to which he was fitting a cover. Before the mill could be stopped the gear had stripped every stitch of clothing from him except his boots, and with that exception he was left as naked as the day he was born, even his shirt being torn from him. Mr. Donelson came out lucky under the circumstances, with a broken rib and a few bruises. His presence of mind was all that saved him from death. When he found himself caught he braced himself by placing a foot against a post and his hands against an elevator. The strain was so hard that he was on the point of giving up when he heard and felt his clothes tearing, and took courage. His clothes had to be cut away from the shaft with a chisel, and altogether it was lucky that there was no mince meat mingled with them.

For those who weren't so lucky, the Balch-Tullis Artificial Limb Company, "Manufacturers of Air Cushion Limbs," advertised various prostheses in its 1928 catalog.

To the person about to order his first limb: there is a world of information to be given the newly amputated prospective wearer of an artificial limb and to him a great deal is confusing as every manufacture extols his own product and infers that the rest of them are not made properly neither are they made of the proper material.

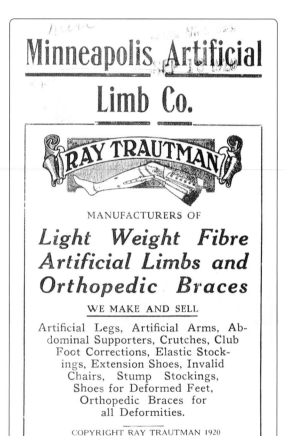

Minneapolis Artificial Limb Co.

RAY TRAUTMAN

MANUFACTURERS OF

Light Weight Fibre Artificial Limbs and Orthopedic Braces

WE MAKE AND SELL

Artificial Legs, Artificial Arms, Abdominal Supporters, Crutches, Club Foot Corrections, Elastic Stockings, Extension Shoes, Invalid Chairs, Stump Stockings, Shoes for Deformed Feet, Orthopedic Braces for all Deformities.

COPYRIGHT RAY TRAUTMAN 1920

240 South Fourth Street
Dean Building
MINNEAPOLIS, MINN.

Corner—Opposite Court House

The Minneapolis Artificial Limb Company advertised its products and services in this 1920 catalog.

It is up to the prospective wearer to read each and every bit of information that he can get on the subject and then try to weed out the true from the false and above all to use his own judgment in the selection of the limb. He has to wear this appliance and he, alone, will be the judge and jury, as no one else will be able to feel for him, he is the one to say whether or not the limb is as it should be, and Comfort is the only real thing that matters. The old style "Peg" leg is far better than one made of gold or silver if it is Comfortable and the other is not.

Our Guarantee
We guarantee in each and every appliance fit, material and workmanship for a period of five years from date of delivery. We obligate ourselves to replace anything that fails to give service, where it can be shown that it is caused either by faulty material or workmanship.

In 1904, E. H. Erickson, himself an amputee, worked at making prostheses in his Minneapolis factory. (Charles J. Hibbard, photo)

Harnessing

THE FALLS

Building a Canal

From their nearly simultaneous incorporation in 1856, the Minneapolis Mill Company had shared waterpower at the falls with its east side neighbor, the St. Anthony Falls Water Power Company. While the Minneapolis company engaged in numerous projects to maximize the power available to industries on the west side, its counterpart spent more than a decade paralyzed by debt and conflict.

The first project undertaken by the Minneapolis Mill Company was construction of a canal that diverted water from the central millpond along a route parallel with the shore. By routing the current to sites just off the riverfront, the canal multiplied the options for harnessing the falls' generous power. Work on the canal began in 1857, as workers blasted through the layer of hard limestone to the soft sandstone beneath and excavated a passage 14 feet deep, 50 feet wide, and 215 feet long. Nine years later, the canal would be extended to 600 feet to accommodate the growing number of mills, and in 1885 it was lengthened to 950 feet and deepened to maximize the waterpower.

The waterway network expanded for several decades; workers here build a canal in 1890. Water was diverted to the canal, shared by mills on both sides, and returned to the river below the falls (right). To further maximize use of precious riverfront space, a railroad trestle was built one level above the plank roadway that covered the canal (above). (Henry R. Farr, photos)

From the *St. Paul Daily Press*, September 21, 1866.

The Canal—Work is being driven rapidly onward. The massive walls of the canal already enclose the spacious trench from Cataract street to the steep bluff below. The heavy explosions in the limestone beds, near Cataract street, startle the visitor at short intervals, and so with powder and levers and the busy hands of men the work goes bravely on. The great walls of the canal will run close up to the mill of Perkins, Crocker & Co. This fine piece of engineering will be the glory of the Falls and of Minneapolis.

From the *Minneapolis Daily Chronicle*, November 22, 1866.

The New Canal at the Mills

This is one of the finest specimens of masonry to be found in the country. The Minneapolis Water-power Company, finding that the supply of water from the old canal could not supply power for more than one-half of the mills which were to be erected, conceived the plan of building a Canal, larger, deeper, and longer, and which should endure for all time. They have dug down into the solid ledge a distance of fifteen feet, and used the huge rocks they have blasted out to make the wall. The new canal commences in the old canal at Cataract Mill and extends thence down parallel with the river, five hundred and seventy-five feet. It is fifty-five feet wide and fifteen feet deep. The wall is three feet thick and solidly cemented, with finely arched gateways. This massive work reflects great credit upon the company for the enterprise as well as upon Franklin Cook, the surveyor and engineer who planned the work. That the work has been well done is shown by the fact that it has cost the large sum of thirty thousand dollars.

The canals brought water close to the mill buildings, but to unleash its energy-producing potential each mill needed its own headraces, wheel pits, and tailraces. The headrace moved water from the canal to the mill, where it turned wheels set in the building's sub-basements. The deeper the wheel pit, the farther the water would fall, and the greater the power yield. Pitched to route the "used" water from under the wheel, the tailrace conducted it back to the canal or into the river below the falls. The Minneapolis Mill Company oversaw the construction of these races, and soon nearly three miles of tunnels and open canals honeycombed the manufacturing district. The company maintained these canals and a dam above the millpond that funneled water to the shore, and it leased land and waterpower separately to milling enterprises. Each company signed a contract stipulating the amount of water it could use in a given period, measured in "millpower," or units of about fifty to sixty horsepower. Not surprisingly, ongoing negotiation was essential to keep each mill running at the appropriate capacity and to ensure that no company infringed on another's right to the waterpower.

Sometimes the Minneapolis Mill Company had to remind its lessees of the rights of other businesses further down the line. Company agent **H. B. Hancock** wrote this letter to saw millers Russell and Huy, whose refuse had apparently been clogging the tunnel.

January 12, 1871

Having heretofore given you notice to remove, without delay the shavings, saw dust and chips now in what is known as the First street Tunnel and in the branch into it from your Mill premises in Minneapolis, you are now notified not to discharge or drop, or allow to be discharged or dropped into said Tunnel from your Mill any more shavings, saw dust or chips, as we will not permit this to be done.

You are also notified that said Tunnel and its branches and the wheel pits to them must be permanently and securely lined without delay by the persons who built or use them, to obviate injury to them and to the property over or near them, and that until these matters are properly done, and to enable them to be done, you must not discharge water into and through said tunnel and the branch leading into it from your mill property.

. . . The Minneapolis Mill Company is now ready to join with you and other parties interested in permanently establishing the size, and lining and protecting said main tunnel from injury and from occasioning injury, and in placing such work in the charge of an Engineer to be agreed upon by us all, or in the charge of Mr. J. T. Stevens. But we will not pay for any part of this work if planned and executed by interested parties, [on the] part of the tunnel owners, or without the services of Mr. Stevens or an Engineer as aforesaid.

. . . We give you this notice in order to avoid any misunderstanding and to have the work undertaken and properly executed without delay.

Water rushes through a tailrace under construction in 1895. Tailraces channeled the "used" current back to the river.

Building an Apron

Although St. Anthony Falls had been viewed as a geological godsend from the time of its earliest settlers, the cascade's power in fact hid its fragility. A thin layer of limestone provided a strong anchor for dams, but that layer rested atop one hundred feet of sandstone. That stone's softness allowed for easy digging of shoreline tunnels and canals, but it also meant that the falls' very foundation was friable and easily dissolved by its own force.

To prevent the falls from deteriorating to a swift running rapids, the Minneapolis Mill Company hired engineer Franklin Cook to build a wooden water slide, or apron, over the western falls. After flooding in 1867 destroyed the half-finished apron, the question turned from whether the falls needed to be protected to who should pay for the work. The Minneapolis Mill Company had lost $35,000 on the project and sought assistance first from its east-bank counterpart, the St. Anthony Company, then from the federal government, and finally from the citizens of Minneapolis and St. Anthony. After much debate, in 1869 citizens agreed to a bonding bill to raise money from the populace and combine it with donations from the mill companies, the falls' most obvious beneficiaries. J. T. Stevens of Lewiston, Maine, was hired to supervise the work. The water-power and the millers' livelihood would be preserved, but at the same time some commentators lamented the further taming of the cataract by human hands.

With an apron protecting the falls, "the people breathed easier and felt that the cities had taken a new lease on life. The apron stands to this day, and will ever stand, if watched and kept in repair," according to Henry T. Welles. This 1870 C. A. Zimmerman postcard image hints at the magnitude of the job.

From the *Minneapolis Tribune*, March 17, 1869.

Minneapolis has spoken. By a vote overwhelming, almost unanimous, she tells the world that there is no backward progress for her. Her motto is Excelsior, *and her course is onward. The Falls are to be improved, protected, saved—made permanent as the everlasting hills. Our water power is no longer in danger, for our citizens,*

With apron construction under way in 1870, this photographer aimed his camera west across the river.
Floods often washed away these wooden aprons, but in 1954 a permanent concrete apron was erected.

*with the characteristic energy which builds up the great cities of the mighty West,
have resolved to meet and oppose the destructive powers of nature herself, and they
know the cunning handiwork that will stay her ceaseless forces and turn them into
channels of industry and make them the servants of man! The Falls will have an
apron, an apron that will extend from shore to shore, an apron that will endure, that
will prevent the wearing away of the rock, turning the tumbling current to a smooth
and gentle flow. The remedy is simple and easy—has been repeatedly and success-
fully employed in cases similar. All that was wanting was the money, and the means
of procuring it are now provided.*

It is a fortunate and auspicious day for Minneapolis. Our destiny is now assured. Our fame is fixed as the future manufacturing metropolis of the Great Northwest. The Dual City will become not merely a Lowell, but the complement of many Lowells. The water power of Lowell is a baby compared to ours. When the great Northwest shall be as densely populated as Massachusetts, Lowell will be a baby city compared to the metropolis at the Falls of St. Anthony!

～～～～～

Walter Stone Pardee arrived in Minnesota from Connecticut in 1866 and earned a degree in civil engineering and architecture from the University of Minnesota. He worked

While appreciating the importance of preserving the falls for industry, many lamented the loss of their swift-running natural beauty.

in the offices of LeRoy S. Buffington, organized the Minneapolis Building Inspection Department, and lent his skills to the Minneapolis Board of Education. His autobiography, written after his retirement in 1910, contains a vivid account of the falls prior to the apron.

My inspiration was the big Falls in high water. There was something awful about them before the days of the "apron." They inspired me with courage. I couldn't get close enough to this immensity of falling water. One seemed willing to die, in some heroic way, when watching the big water drop into the pit. Hearing its majestic roar and seeing it swirl and tumble away like the water in the whirlpool of Niagara itself. There was no sense nor fear of danger, but rather an uncanny attraction toward it all, and in the great flood of 1867; so high that I laid on the floor of the Suspension bridge and touched the water with [my] hand; so high that West Side mill platforms were two feet afloat; and the flumes to carry boards away down the river for rafting, were swaying and washing out, where they crossed the whirlpool; there was one boy at least who must run down those tottering flumes to the very end. However he got back I'm sure I don't know. There was but one thought in mind: the awful grandeur of it all. This was a great privilege to get away from the humdrum of life and into the swirl.

~~~~~

From the *Minneapolis Tribune*, August 12, 1869.

The Falls—The work of improving the Falls is now being pushed forward with great energy. The blasting is mostly completed, and a large crew of men are now at work building the foundation of the apron. They have commenced at the foot of the Falls, and are building a solid frame work of logs, the interstices being filled with immense rocks, and the whole when completed to be covered with two thicknesses of heavy timbers. This frame-work will extend clear across the river, and will run down nearly 200 feet in length. Three immense derricks have been put up, to be used in lifting the heavy rocks into position, and the work is now getting in such shape that rapid progress can be made.

Now is the time for all those who wish to take a final look at old St. Anthony Falls in its natural condition. Its natural beauty, of which poets and writers throughout the world have said so much, will soon be gone forever, and nothing will be left but a continuation of rapids, made by the great apron. It is a stupendous work to accomplish; yet engineering skill, accompanied with men and money, will overcome all obstacles, and so the mighty Falls of St. Anthony have been made to succumb to man, and are now as subject to his will as a child.

Tunnel Collapse

William W. Eastman and **John L. Merriam** bought Nicollet Island in 1865 from the St. Anthony Falls Water Power Company. But, due to carelessness on the firm's part, the deed for the land did not exclude the waterpower rights, of which the company had long believed itself to be the

William W. Eastman settled in St. Anthony in 1854 and was instrumental in the development of Minnesota's lumber industry, woolen and paper mills, and early railroads.

sole owner. Capitalizing on this blunder, the new owners demanded that the dams and other installations be removed from their island, possibly hoping to force the company to buy back the land at an inflated price. The company responded with a new contract to share the waterpower,

Arriving in Minnesota in 1860, John L. Merriam ran a staging and express business with J. C. Burbank and Captain Russell Blakeley. He helped to organize the First National Bank and the Merchants' National Bank of St. Paul and in 1870 served as a representative in the state legislature.

including a clause permitting Eastman and Merriam to build a tunnel under Hennepin and Nicollet Islands as a tailrace to carry away the used water. This plan would have greatly increased the east side industrial area served by waterpower and was met with much enthusiasm by the Minneapolis and St. Anthony press. Disaster struck on October 4, 1869, however, when during the tunnel excavation the thin top layer of limestone was breached, causing a leak that turned into a torrent and nearly destroyed the falls.

~~~~~

From the *Minneapolis Tribune*, September 16, 1868.

An Important Enterprise

Tunnelling Under Hennepin and Nicollet Islands

Their Banks to be Lined with Manufacturing Establishments

Perhaps few of our citizens while looking upon the numerous manufacturing establishments at the Falls, and listening to the incessant clatter of the busy machinery, have for an instant dreamed of seeing the substantial walls of similar establishments rising upon Nicollet Island, and that locality, now so quiet, converted into a manufacturing centre second only to the Falls themselves. Such a result is to be accomplished, however, and at no distant day. Messrs. W. W. Eastman and John L. Merriam have engaged in the important enterprise of cutting a tunnel from the foot of Hennepin Island to within one hundred feet of Bridge street, Nicollet Island, a distance of 2,650 feet, ten feet more than half a mile; and when completed, that portion of the Island below Bridge street, about eight acres in extent, will be quite as available for manufacturing purposes as any locality above the Falls.

Henry T. Welles settled in Minnesota in 1853 to pursue his interests in lumber and real estate. Instrumental in the development of Minneapolis, he served as the first mayor of St. Anthony and was a Democratic candidate for governor in 1863. He vividly recalled the tunnel disaster in his *Autobiography and Reminiscence*, published in 1899.

The Falls of St. Anthony, it was thought, were about to disappear, the great manu-facturing future, which the optimistic imagination of vigorous youth had painted for the cities by the falls was fading away. Men saw in imagination a ruined water power, crushed hopes, the loss of large investments, and a deserted city.

. . . it was plain that the erosion of this volume of water would soon undermine the limestone bed of the river, which, falling in, would ruin the falls and replace them by a series of rapids.

One tunnel too many: Eastman and Merriam's tunnel endangered the lives and livelihoods of those who depended on the falls. Thirty years later, this underground worker was presumably engaged in a less volatile project.

To add to the terrors of the situation the waters rushing out through the mouth of the tunnel attacked the lower end of Hennepin island with Titanic force. At one moment a triangular piece of the island measuring one hundred and fifty feet fell into the roaring waters. The total destruction of the island was regarded as imminent. By this time the fire department came to the rescue, a general alarm was sounded, and the entire population of the two cities of Minneapolis and St. Anthony rushed to the island or lined the banks and bridges. All of the mills of Hennepin island, the Summit flouring mill, the River mills, the Island mill and the paper mill were regarded as doomed. Scores of teams and hundreds of men went to work removing from them all that was movable.

"Disaster confronted the cities. . . . The torrent went down under Hennepin island, undermined a portion of the island, wrecking several buildings. The people rushed *en masse* to the rescue," recalled Henry T. Welles.

But calamity followed calamity in close succession. While the men were yet working on the island a large section of it over the tunnel caved in with one team and a score of men, though, happily all made their escape. It is hard to find words to depict the situation at this moment. Above was the roaring, whirling maelstrom which threatened to absorb the whole river, further down the tunnel was caving in and the battering waters were tearing Hennepin island to pieces, rolling great rocks into the stream as though they were shavings.

. . . the hundreds and even thousands of volunteers, with scores and scores of teams sent by every mill in the city began the work of stopping the gap. Brush, dirt, stones, logs, timber and trees were thrown into the maw of the river and swallowed up like egg shells. The men worked all day with no decrease in energy or diminution in determination to win—but all the debris thrown in to the maelstrom was engulfed as though it were so much snow. Mighty logs and giant sticks of timber were tossed around, thrown up in the air and then drawn down out of sight by a force that snapped them off like pipe stems. Not only did the river laugh in contemptuous scorn at the efforts made to subdue it, but it extended its operations further and further, ever enlarging the great hole in the bottom.

Baffled in their first attempt, the leaders took council and decided to attack the monster in another way. It was determined to build a big raft, float it over the chasm and sink it. Fortunately, Nicollet island was covered with heavy timber, which a thousand milling hands had soon converted into a big raft. This raft was swung around over the opening and firmly anchored. Then, with feverish haste, loads of dirt and stone were hauled out from Nicollet island, together with brush and debris of every sort that would tend to stop the water. The work progressed finely, the raft settled down into the gap, and at length it seemed as though man's cunning had triumphed over the river. The teams came and went, the earth on the raft was piled up until it rose several feet above the baffled waters.

The men who had toiled with such fierce energy strolled up and down the embankment their hands had raised and glanced exultingly at the roaring waters, which seemed to be snarling in defeat. The workers were still congratulating each other when to the horror of the spectators the great raft went down in the center. It seemed that the river was about to take the lives of a hundred for their attempt to curb its will. A panic seized those on the raft, but fortunately the sunken part rose again and gave an opportunity for all to escape to the shore. Then it was seen that another big section of the limestone near the shore of the island had given away. In a short time the raft was a useless pile of debris, merely a sieve through which the waters poured in ever-increasing volume.

From the *St. Anthony Falls Democrat*, October 15, 1869.

The break instead of ruining will save us. It will arouse the people not only of these cities but of the whole country to a sense of the situation. In looking at the falls as they are to-day, and thinking of them as old settlers say they were fifteen years ago, it appears astonishing that nothing was done to preserve them, and nothing effectual attempted until the year of our Lord 1869. Before the eyes of those most deeply interested, they have receded from year to year. There was a vague indefinite feeling that something some time might have to be done—little more. Now it is demonstrated that something must *be done, and done immediately. The result will be that* sufficient *will be done, which would not otherwise have been the case. If it costs half a million these falls will at last be protected, so that greater confidence, and greater prosperity than ever will come to these cities.*

To preserve St. Anthony Falls, men worked for months to build a dam that would funnel the water away from the tunnel and prevent further harm. The next year, James B. Francis, an engineer from Lowell, Massachusetts, assessed the damage and recommended that the apron be completed (work on it had been interrupted by the disaster), the tunnel be sealed, and low dams be built above the falls to maintain a protective layer of water over the limestone at all times. Because destruction of the falls could affect navigation on the river below, the federal government stepped in to complete the work of preservation. By 1884, not only was the apron complete and the tunnel sealed, but a dike protected the sandstone from water seepage, two low dams kept a steady current over the limestone, and a new sluiceway carried logs more safely over the falls. All told, the government spent $615,000, with the cities submitting an additional $334,500, over fourteen years to preserve navigation on the upper river. The livelihoods of Minneapolis and St. Anthony were assured.

A cleanup crew surveys the damage after the tunnel break in an effort headlined "The Prompt Action of Our People" by the *Minneapolis Tribune*. (Beal's Gallery, photo)

From "The Flour-Mills of Minneapolis," by Eugene V. Smalley.

The pictures of the Falls of St. Anthony which most of us remember to have admired in the school geographies bear no sort of resemblance to the real falls of to-day. There are no forests now, no island, and no rocks, and in place of the wild fall there

Various projects at the falls combined with the destruction caused by the tunnel break and later flooding resulted in significant changes to the riverfront's appearance. Picturesque views aside, a concerned citizenry wished to see waterpower preserved whatever the cost. (Whitney and Zimmerman, photo)

is only a planked water-slide that looks like a mill-dam—an enormous and magnificent mill-dam, truly, but nevertheless a mill-dam. The whole sweep of the fall has been covered with an "apron" of planks to prevent the rocks from being worn away, and to save the cataract from being converted into a rapid. The real dam, a short distance above the falls, affords power to numerous saw-mills, and within it there is a boom to catch logs. In the winter and spring the falls, thus tamed and fettered, are still very beautiful, the rush of waters over the symmetrical curve of the dam affording a striking spectacle; but in summer, when most of the volume of the current is taken out to feed the mill-races, there is little to be seen but an imposing structure of dry planks.

RAILROADS

Located at a geographic intersection between east and west, Minneapolis drew major rail lines to its industrial district, and these quickly spread beyond the city's limits. In the 1870s and 1880s, railroad building and land settling complemented each other: towns grew up near railroad corridors that served the population by conveniently bringing in manufactured goods and shipping out agricultural products. In this period, railroad companies were major promoters of farms and town sites along their routes, their ultimate goal to move filled boxcars to eastern manufacturers.

On a local scale, rail transportation was integral to the industries at the falls, bringing in wheat and timber and shipping out flour and lumber. The first railroads to connect with St. Anthony and Minneapolis arrived in the mid-1860s. In 1863, the St. Paul and Pacific Railroad built a line to the east side of St. Anthony, and in 1865 the Minnesota Central began operating just west of the mill district. With these rail lines Minneapolis was linked to the east via Chicago, another city where flour milling was a significant industry. Local millers soon found themselves at a disadvantage, however, as Chicago lines were able to set freight rates that were meant to drive Minneapolis out of the market. To remedy the situation, Minneapolis millers financed the Minneapolis, St. Paul and Sault Ste. Marie Railroad (Soo Line), which linked up with the Canadian Pacific Railway and allowed them to bypass Chicago and ship directly to eastern markets beginning in 1888.

Three decades later, nine major railroads served Minneapolis and hundreds of freight and passenger trains entered the city daily. Rail service was at its peak, but the milling industry it served was beginning to decline. Soon rail traffic in the mill district would drop dramatically.

When future railroad magnate **James J. Hill** arrived in St. Paul in 1856, he worked as a shipping clerk for J. W. Bass and Company. He soon set his sights high: his dream was to build a rail line to the Pacific. By 1866 he was on his way, serving as general manager and president of the St. Paul and Pacific Railroad, which he reorganized as the St. Paul, Minneapolis and Manitoba in

"Empire builder" James J. Hill envisioned railroads reaching throughout the Northwest.

1879. He became president of the St. Anthony Falls Water Power Company in 1882 and worked to improve water use efficiency on the east side. But rather than directly promoting industry at the falls, he concentrated on his growing railroad empire, by which western wheat farmers shipped their products to Minneapolis. Hill also built the Stone Arch Bridge over the Mississippi River to connect east and west, and his Minneapolis Union Railway Company financed the bustling Union Depot, conveniently located just blocks from the mill district. Hill's dream was realized in 1890, when rails were expanded to the Pacific and the St. Paul, Minneapolis and Manitoba and its linking tracks were renamed the Great Northern Railway.

The Stone Arch Bridge, straddling the Mississippi River to carry the cars of the St. Paul, Minneapolis and Manitoba road, was an unmistakable landmark for the mill district. Built entirely of stone, the bridge still stands 2,100 feet long, 28 feet wide, and 82 feet tall, with twenty-three arches each spanning from forty to one hundred feet. At first dubbed "Hill's Folly," the bridge required three years and $650,000 to build: it was opened on November 22, 1883.

Charles C. Smith was the architect for the Stone Arch Bridge and the chief engineer for the Great Northern Railway. His report, "Stone Railway Viaduct Across the Mississippi River at Minneapolis Built during 1882 and 1883," explains its diagonal placement across the waterway.

Location

The approach from the East rendered an oblique crossing of the River necessary. . . . The present site—just below the Falls—was adopted for the following reasons: The absolute safety of the bridge from ice or log jams, the comparative inexpensive and permanent foundation, the best approach and entry to the Union Depot grounds on the West bank of the River, the views from the bridge of the Falls of St. Anthony, the suspension and other bridges, the mills and large portion of the city of Minneapolis on one side, while on the other a long stretch of the Mississippi River, deep in its gorge, reaching away towards St. Paul, would tend to make the Railway lines using this route more attractive to travelers.

From the *St. Paul and Minneapolis Pioneer Press,* November 17, 1883.

A Stroll in Mid-Air

Starting from the extremity of the bridge on the west side, just below, or, rather, behind the Cararact mill,

the massive stone work stretches to the east across the river, curving at first slightly to the left in a graceful sweep until a point is reached directly below the outer end of the platform where its course straightens and runs thence in a right line directly to the landing place on the East side at the foot of Sixth avenue southeast, the whole course being 2,100 feet. The upper surface of the bridge presents to the view a smooth stone roadway carrying two tracks on four lines of steel rails and walled in on either side by heavy blocks of stone, high enough and strong enough to prevent a train from leaving the bridge even should it be derailed, a matter of much consequence where trains are to be run at full speed over sixty feet up in the air. . . .

One of the most comprehensive views of the city and falls that can be had is from the roadway of the bridge; the entire milling district on both banks, the suspension bridge, the commanding public buildings, the falls, the apron, with its picturesque coating of ice and snow, the State university, the noble sweep of the river below the mouth of Tuttle's creek; all the beauties and business of the city spread out before the gaze of incoming travelers. The value of such an approach to Minneapolis as an advertisement can hardly be estimated.

From the *Daily Minnesota Tribune,* November 23, 1883.

The Great Bridge

This viaduct, which has now been nearly three years in building, is the only one of its kind that spans the Father of Waters, and is one of the longest and most noteworthy in the United States. Firmer than the earth which supports it, it is constructed to stand the test of time until the golden age shall arrive when the problem of aerial navigation shall have been solved, and railroads and railroad bridges will be useless works of engineering.

Facing page: In 1900, the majestic Stone Arch Bridge pointed to the west side mills as it angled across the river below the falls. With such a view, train passengers would not have questioned Minneapolis's reputation as a "mill city."

Hydroelectricity

The first hydroelectric station in the United States was built at St. Anthony Falls in 1882 and operated by the Minnesota Brush Electric Company. By using waterpower to generate electricity, then distributing it widely, this plant offered the most efficient use of the falls' energy. A small frame building on Upton Island contained five Brush arc-light machines that transmitted power from a waterwheel through circuits to businesses on Washington Avenue. On September 5, 1882, the lights at this central station were turned on for the first time, just twenty-five days ahead of the nation's second hydroelectric station, in Appleton, Wisconsin. Within a few years, electric lights illuminated the streets of Minneapolis, phasing out gas lamps despite early fears concerning the safety of overhead current-carrying wires. But the Brush Electric Company utilized waterpower for just two years, after which it moved upstream to Third Avenue North and converted its operations to steam, at the time a more reliable power source than the water levels at the falls, which fluctuated with the seasons.

"No action could long delay the introduction of light into Minneapolis," noted the *Minneapolis Tribune*. Soaring 250 feet high, the city's first electric streetlight had eight 400-candlepower lamps. Ironically, the streetlight was too tall to meet its goal of illuminating the entire downtown.

Minneapolis General Electric, a successor company of Minnesota Brush Electric, began renting excess water—that unused by the mills at the falls—in 1894 and soon had consolidated the property and water rights previously held by the east side sawmills. In 1894–95, the company built its Main Street Station and began generating 8,000 horsepower, nearly 6,000 kilowatts.

~~~~~

From the *Daily Pioneer Press*, August 3, 1881.

The Electric Light in the Pillsbury A Mill

The Brush electric light, which is used for lighting the Pillsbury A mill, was started last evening and promises to be a grand success. The sixteen lights which are now running present a beautiful appearance and make the mill lighter than it is at noonday. Two of the lights are in the basement, four on the first floor, and two on each of the five succeeding floors. The lights are enclosed in globes, perfectly dust-tight, and are about the size and shape of gas lamps. The light from each one is intense in its brightness and [so] clear that the finest shades of colors can be readily distinguished. In company with Mr. G. M. Hoag, the electrician, under whose supervision the lights were put in, the machinery connected with the lights was inspected. The dynamo electric machine, which is run by the water power and generates the electricity, occupies a space only six by four feet. . . . This is the only flouring mill in the world where the light is in use, but it is undoubtedly only a question of time when it will be used in all of the mills. . . . The effect of the lights as they shone from the windows of the immense structure was beautiful, and during the evening a large number of people, attracted by the illumination, visited the mill.

From the *Minneapolis Tribune*, March 17, 1882.

"It has been thoroughly demonstrated," said [Brush company secretary] Mr. King, "by practical experience in New York, Philadelphia, Boston, and many other cities in the Untied States that no danger whatever to life, limb or property attaches in the introduction of the Brush system with the wire on poles, and it is so introduced in every city in this country where the electric lights burn, so far as my knowledge extends. . . . Minneapolis is the only city that has refused to allow the introduction of the coming light. . . . We expect as part of our system to introduce the best incandescent light ever seen in this or any other country. It's a beauty and beats them all!"

Minneapolis General Electric built its Main Street Station at the falls in 1894. A series of mergers led to the creation in 1916 of Northern States Power, which operated a station on the site until 1968. The building is now owned by Xcel Energy.

In 1889 the two waterpower companies, Minneapolis Mill and St. Anthony Falls Water Power, were purchased by the Pillsbury-Washburn Flour Mills Company, Ltd. The companies remained separate in name, so as not to jeopardize the contracts each had signed with various manufacturers, but they were united by a common engineer, William de la Barre, who already had a decade of experience at the falls. With the energy output of the entire waterfall now in the hands of one company and with innovations introduced by de la Barre, the remaining hydropower capacity at the falls could be developed to generate electricity for the mill district and beyond.

William de la Barre was an engineer trained in Austria who immigrated to the United States in 1867. In Philadelphia he learned to build steam, gas, and waterworks machinery, and in 1878 he arrived in Minneapolis and helped construct the new Washburn mill. De la Barre was named engineer for the Minneapolis Milling Company in 1883. Adopting a scientific approach with an eye toward the future, he worked with the mills to harness the current to its full advantage, negotiated with the St. Anthony Falls Water Power Company to share the power, and observed the water flow for years to understand

Austrian engineer William de la Barre worked tirelessly to maximize the power supplied by St. Anthony Falls.

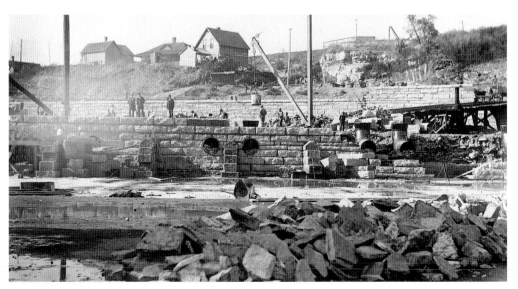

The Lower Dam was completed in 1897 to increase waterpower available on the east side.

how its capacity could be maximized. He instituted many policies that increased its potential: he improved dams, maintained millpond levels, convinced manufacturers to increase the "head" or vertical distance of the water's drop upon their wheels, and held companies to the water limits stated in their leases (for years firms had taken as much as they could get, with little concern for the effect on the falls or on mills downstream). With de la Barre's genius and the work of many others, careful water management and hydro-electricity increased the energy harnessed at the falls from 13,000 horsepower in the 1880s to 55,068 in 1908.

The Lower Dam Hydro Plant, strikingly modern even in this 1895 view, powered streetcars until the 1950s, when it became part of Northern States Power. The building and dam washed away in 1987 when the sandstone layer beneath it was scoured out.

The Lower Dam, completed in 1897, was designed and built under the auspices of William de la Barre to harness the energy of the twenty-foot drop below the falls. Costing nearly one million dollars to build, the dam funneled water to the east bank power station for Thomas Lowry's streetcar company, Twin City Rapid Transit. With a 10,000-horsepower capacity, the plant converted water into electricity that mobilized the streetcars of Minneapolis and St. Paul. Twin City Rapid Transit leased the Lower Dam plant until 1950, when its operations shifted from electric-powered streetcars to buses.

The Twin City Rapid Transit Company steam plants, including one at the Lower Dam and this one at Third Avenue North and Second Street, powered "the best system of electric roads in the country." (Henry B. Herington, photo)

Thomas Lowry arrived in Minneapolis in 1867 and pursued interests in law and real estate. His uncommon vision would soon focus on public transportation, from horse-drawn carriages to streetcars. In 1878 he was named president of the Minneapolis Street Railway Company, and soon after he campaigned to introduce electric-powered streetcars in Minneapolis. Many expressed safety concerns, but Lowry persevered, working to increase the ease and speed of transportation between and within Minneapolis and St. Paul through the Twin City Rapid Transit Company, incorporated in 1891. Just eight years later, the electric streetcars were carrying 175,000 passengers daily. By the time of Lowry's death in 1909, streetcars could travel the forty-eight miles between Excelsior and Stillwater, and Minneapolis and St. Paul were crisscrossed with 368 miles of track.

"Mr. Streetcar": Thomas Lowry dedicated himself to public transportation in the Twin Cities.

At a celebratory banquet in 1892, **Archbishop John Ireland** spoke in praise of Thomas Lowry and the Twin City Rapid Transit Company.

Your work! It is visible to all eyes. Words are not needed from me to make it known. Not two years have yet gone by, since the first car moved by the electric spark, sped over our streets. Heretofore, apart from two or three short lines of cable, we had been going our way as the slow pace of the wan and weather-beaten street-horse led us. The first day of last March bade farewell to the last horse-car. Today we have in Minneapolis and St. Paul 215 miles of cable, and electric lines. One thousand cars journey speedily over them, covering ground at the rate of 8 or 21 miles per hour, as the freedom of the thoroughfare permits. Only a few steps from his home need the traveler go to spy a car, and be whirled by it near to any point in either of the two cities. From the farthest part of one he can journey to the most distant part of the other, 20 miles or more, and the highest fare he is required to pay in sweeping over this widest territory is one single dime. Whatever its size no one city in America has so many miles of electric lines as Minneapolis and St. Paul. Indeed, if I am to credit an article in the December number of the Cosmopolitan Review, *we have today in our two cities an electric mileage nearly equal to that in all other American cities united. No large city, outside of our own two, has as yet been able to discard its horse cars. We have the best system of electric roads in the country.*

In 1923, Northern States Power bought the hydroelectric plants at the Lower Dam and on Hennepin Island from Pillsbury Flour Mills Company. Eventually, as the flour milling industry declined, NSP would concentrate the falls' power to produce hydroelectricity.

The conductor and staff of an open streetcar strike a jaunty pose during the summer of 1894.

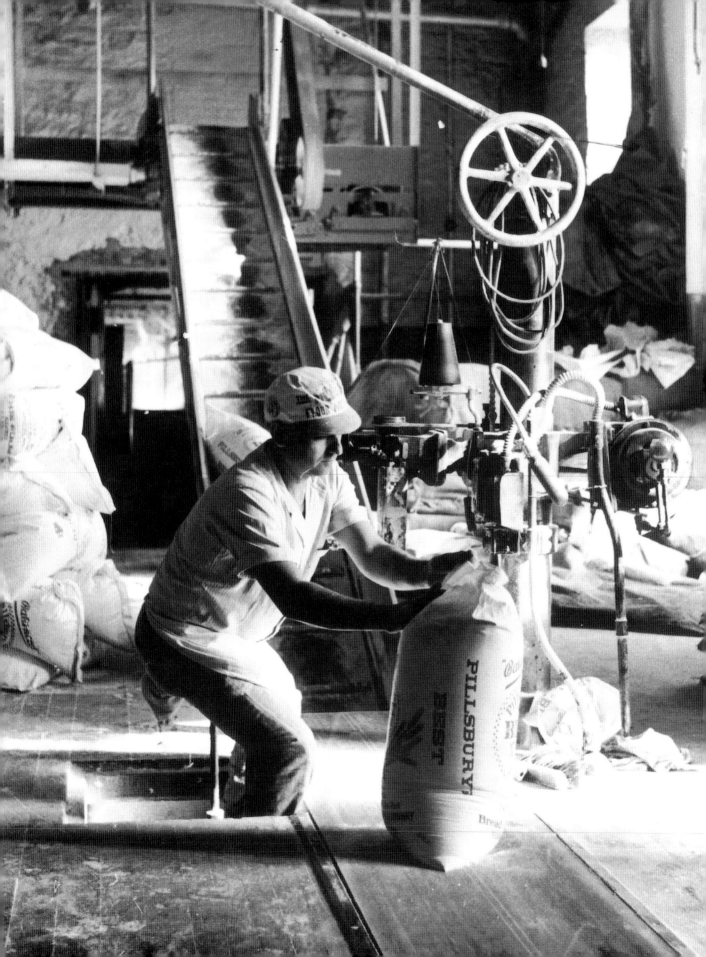

Flour Milling

AT THE FALLS

Improvements in the Milling Process

From the *St. Anthony Express*, February 17, 1855.

Flour from the Minnesota Mills—We acknowledge the receipt of a sack of flour from the Minnesota Flouring Mill at this place. It is fine and soft as any flour we ever saw, and excepting a slightly dark color, is superior to our best imported brands. The specimen sent us is made from the White Bald variety, and though not so white and beautiful in appearance, is superior in quality, we should judge, to that made from the Red River wheat. The time is not distant when Minnesota, with the superiority of her soil and seasons for wheat culture, and her unparalleled water power for manufacturing flour, will export largely of this article. . . . our mills will turn out wheat, superior in quality and appearance to any now manufactured in the West.

The predictions of the *Express* proved prescient, for by 1876 eighteen flour mills had been built below the falls on the west side. The first mills were built on a small scale and used traditional millstones, run at high speeds, to pulverize the grain and produce as much flour as possible in one grinding. However, early Minneapolis millers found themselves competing with mills in other cities for prized winter wheat, which was easily ground into preferred white flour. More readily available from the wheat fields of the Northwest was spring wheat, the kernels of which were very hard and ill suited to the traditional milling process. The resulting product—discolored and easily spoiled—was considered far inferior to winter-wheat flour.

Before the innovations that revolutionized the industry, flour milling had followed centuries-old traditions. Francis and Ichabod Hill of the Minnesota Flouring Mill posed with an obsolescent millstone in 1860.

HUSTON'S
Middlings Purifier.
A SYSTEM OF REELS.
THE SIMPLEST WAY IN THE WORLD
TO PURIFY MIDDLINGS.

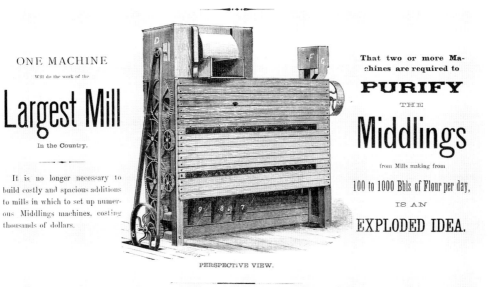

PERSPECTIVE VIEW.

ONE MACHINE

Will do the work of the

Largest Mill

In the Country.

It is no longer necessary to build costly and spacious additions to mills in which to set up numerous Middlings machines, costing thousands of dollars.

That two or more Machines are required to

PURIFY

THE

Middlings

from Mills making from

100 to 1000 Bbls of Flour per day,

IS AN

EXPLODED IDEA.

FACTS FOR CONSIDERATION.

MILLERS: It is a fact worth your earnest consideration, that for separating the flour from the feed and the feed from the middlings nothing has ever superseded revolving reels, nor has any apparatus been discovered, so simple, convenient and effectual. Now that it has been found exceedingly profitable, and at the same time quite practicable, to carry the separations still further, viz: to take the fibrous, dust, fuzz and other speculæ from the pure middlings, does it not seem reasonable that revolving reels, properly clothed and constructed, and with the proper application of air currents, can still be relied upon? Is it common sense to discard the very apparatus that has proved itself to be peculiarly adapted to that kind of work?

The great object desired and persistently sought for by the patentees of the numerous devices, applied to the "shaker" or "jigger" purifiers for keeping the cloths from clogging, is to make out of a FLAT BOLT or SIEVE what the reel of itself is.

☞ Would it not be well to consider what would be the fate of the SIEVE or FLAT BOLT PURIFIERS in case you were milling damp tough wheat, instead of the extremely dry wheat you are now milling?

J. E. HUSTON & CO.,

READ THE OTHER SIDE

Aurora, Kane Co., Ill.

"Released from its long slumber, the spirit of milling progress made giant strides forward, invention succeeded invention, change followed change, and one improvement trod so rapidly on the heels of another that at one time it seemed as if he who would keep up with the progress of the craft must rebuild his plant annually," wrote William C. Edgar. One of these improvements: a middlings purifier advertised by J. E. Hurston and Company.

In the 1870s the Minneapolis millers sought to solve this problem by adapting milling processes that had been developed in Europe and practiced by millers in southern Minnesota. Termed "gradual reduction," this technique revolutionized the industry. First, millstones were replaced by porcelain or iron roller mills, which required fewer repairs and less space than the traditional millstones and were used to produce superior flour through several grindings of the wheat. The second step in this process involved the "middlings purifier." Known as "middlings," the wheat's nutritious layer just under the husk had previously yielded low-grade, bran-speckled flour when ground. In the new process, the middlings were blasted with air in a system of sieves, a technique that removed the light weight bran particles and resulted in a fine white flour with a high gluten content.

This process was already in place in cities like Budapest, where most of the work was done by hand. Minneapolis millers automated the process by adopting machinery that would produce quality flour. As a result of these innovations, a barrel of Minneapolis flour was estimated to yield 12.5 percent more bread than the best winter-wheat flours, and spring wheat was eagerly sought by companies who wished to produce "the best bread-making flour of the world." The city's millers were poised to elevate their product to the number-one spot in the country.

~~~~~~

Franklin Martin came to Minneapolis at age fifteen to work for his uncle, Adolphus Guilder, an inventor and manufacturer of milling machinery. Martin later became a medical doctor, and in his autobiography, *The Joy of Living*, he told of his work in the rapidly changing flour mills of the early 1870s.

> *My first duty was to act as "handy man" to a group of men who were placing the new machine in the Pillsbury plants. The flour mills at that time ignored the accumulation of the dangerous dust which was later identified as the insulating material that caused the destructive explosions. Hence the floor, walls, and machinery of the mills in which we worked were covered by several inches of this fine, gray, impalpable dust.*
>
> *We were placing hundreds of machines in the mills, literally acres of them. It was my duty to aid in whatever job presented itself. It was a new experience. The mystery of machinery was fascinating. The new machines, like many inventions involving fundamental principles, were very simple. Now and again someone would say, "Why didn't someone discover the principle earlier?" The simple device, a graduated set of sieves, separated the hitherto wasted middlings into a finer and yet finer grade. The finest grade formed the basis of the whitest and finest flour, hitherto wasted or used for animal fodder. The coarser grades were reground and again treated by the*

machines, leaving only the coarsest bran with practically no food value. It was an evolution in wheat grinding and flour making, and a great economic saving.

~~~~~~~

From the December 27, 1899, issue of the *Northwestern Miller,*
a reminiscence by W. D. Gray titled "A Quarter-Century of Milling."

Of course there were many, both millers and mill-furnishers, who were prophesying failure, and that we would yet return to the old millstones. They would not change their old set notions to conform to the new condition of things, but were contented to wait and let others do the experimenting. However, the millers who first put in the rolls and the mill-builders who were the first to adopt the roller process and build mills to conform to the new conditions of things, were the men who made the most money. While their more contented brothers in business were waiting until things were perfected, and experimenting was done with, the more progressive millers and mill-furnishers were coining money as they have never done since.

"Everything is automatic." Automation of the industry meant fewer workers and cheaper production. Soon everyone could afford the pure white flour manufactured by the Pillsbury and Washburn-Crosby Companies. A miller grinds wheat into flour, 1895.

IRONWORKS

Although not driven by waterpower, several ironworks industries also rose at the falls and contributed to the success of the lumber and flour milling industries there. Their convenient location allowed mill owners to test ideas and refine prototypes before installing new machinery in their mills. Most ironworks, from foundries to tool factories and machine shops, were built on the east side of the river, close to their customers. These plants supplied basic mill equipment as well as the machinery needed to run the factories. Their strongest presence at the falls was between the 1860s and the 1880s, after which many ironworks relocated away from the waterfront and in some cases away from the cities.

From the *Minneapolis Tribune*, January 7, 1868.

North Star Iron Works

The boring mill, on the first floor is the largest west of Chicago. The foundry occupies a building fifty feet square, and has a capacity of 8 tons a day, and in the pattern shop only the most experienced and careful workers are employed. . . . Twenty one men are employed, all expert workmen, nearly all the work turned out is made to order and first class work is required. . . . The firm are prepared to manufacture steam engines, portable and stationary steam and gas fittings, gang, circular saws, flouring mill machinery, shafting, gears and pulleys, window caps and sills, water wheels, sash weights, &c., also railroad work and architectural building columns.

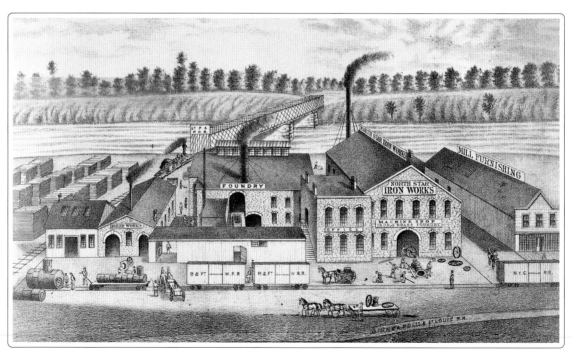

North Star Iron Works of Minneapolis built machinery and tools to order.

In 1857, millwright **Otis A. Pray** moved to Minneapolis, where he specialized in flour mill machinery, constructing mills for William W. Eastman and Cadwallader C. Washburn and installing the first roller mills in the Northwest. Demand for his talents expanded, and in 1878 he built the Minneapolis Iron Works, which eventually

Otis A. Pray and his ironworks were integral to mechanical advancements at the falls.

also produced saw milling machinery. Despite its early success, the company would be consumed by financial failure in 1886.

From the *Minneapolis Tribune*, September 27, 1878.

A Great Industry: The Growth and Importance of the Manufacture of Mill Machinery

All the wonderful power of mechanism, which lifts and moulds and shapes great masses of dormant iron into forms of utility is displayed in its fullest accomplishments. Great planing machines shave down plates of iron as they would some board; great knives whittle from long bars of iron curling shavings, and great gimblets walk through great wheels as though they were cheese. In the moulding and casting room, on days devoted to the purpose, may be seen the cauldrons of sparkling, sputtering, moulton iron, poured into their bed of dirt, to be unearthed as great solid wheels, or pulleys, or plates; or the thousand and one other things of different shapes that go to make up a mill. There is everywhere the evidence of a great, crowding, pushing, prosperous industry; such a one as we may well be proud of, and are in all probability. . . . It is gratifying, though, to know that it has been built up by a gentleman who has been identified with Minneapolis from the earliest day [Mr. O. A. Pray]. . . . At the present time Messrs. O. A. Pray & Co. find themselves so crowded with work under contract and otherwise that they are obliged to turn away work which they are unable to do.

Employees take a break at Minneapolis Iron Works, ca. 1915.

BONANZA FARMS

Minnesota's economy was doubly blessed: just as the falls was a prime location for milling industries, the state's soil was particularly appropriate for raising the wheat that would feed the flour mills. When land became available in 160-acre parcels by decree of the 1862 Homestead Act, settlers poured into the territory, dug up the rich prairie soil, and planted acres and acres of wheat. Demand for Minnesota and Dakota wheat grew, and fields were consolidated into privately-owned "bonanza farms" covering thousands of acres, committed to producing "Number 1 Hard" spring wheat. As milling industries developed, the various middlemen grasped at farmers' profits, and smaller farms especially were at the mercy of grain elevator managers who often graded the wheat so low that farmers could not recover the year's expenses. Bonanza farmers, operating on an industrial scale yielding thousands of bushels, were better able to challenge grain grading and shipping rates, but this option was not available to diversified farmers operating on the Jeffersonian ideal.

G. W. Schatzel chronicled his visit to Minnesota's booming farmland in the essay "Among the Wheat-Fields of Minnesota," which was published in *Harper's New Monthly Magazine* in 1868.

Minnesota is pre-eminently the wheat growing State of the Union. . . . Owing to the peculiarity of her climate and soil, she is the best adapted of any of the States to the raising of this staple. Wheat is in fact almost her exclusive object of production. None farm here except for this. Her dry, clear, and, for the most part, cool atmosphere makes Minnesota the very paradise of wheat-growers. As one stands on the boundless rolling prairies of this country, and looks around him on every side, and sees the interminable reach of slightly undulating soil, clad with golden-rod, fire-weed, and a vast variety of other flowering plants, intermixed with prairie-grass, and notices the almost utter absence of forest, and catches the onward rush of the fresh, cool southern breeze that sweeps by with a voluminous force, he involuntarily thinks of the wide expanse of the ocean, and snuffs the wind as he would the sea-breeze itself. . . .

But dreams and imagination can not last long in this intensely practical country, as it is to-day. You have only to cast your eye across the prairie, and you see farms yellow with the golden grain which forms the wealth of this rapidly-growing young State. The illusion fades away; civilized life, with all its rush and bustle, comes before you, and you see the farmer guiding his reaper through the standing wheat, followed by his "hands," stooping over and binding their bosomfuls of swaths. And who, although poetry suffers, can regret the change?

"The prairie lay golden-green and endless as a sea. No buildings could be seen, with the exception of our own barns and sleeping shed in the midst of the fields. Not a tree, not a bush grew there—only wheat and grass, wheat and grass, as far as the eye could see," wrote bonanza farm laborer Knut Hamsun in 1887. Workers harvest acres of wheat near the Red River Valley, 1900 (left), and a farmer poses with his wheat crop in Aitkin County, 1910 (above). (Harry Darius Ayer, photo)

Mary Dodge Woodward lived on a 1,500-acre bonanza wheat farm in the Red River Valley from 1882 until 1888. A fifty-six-year-old widow, she moved from Wisconsin with her grown sons and a daughter. She recorded her experiences among the vast wheat fields in diaries published after her death as *The Checkered Years: A Bonanza Farm Diary, 1884–1888.*

July 10, 1884
Nobody can imagine how beautiful the wheat fields look, whole sections without a break waving in the breeze. What would the old Vermonters say of it? I wish they could see Cass County now, just as it stands, one vast ocean of wheat.

January 18, 1885
We are quite protected here. Our buildings shelter somewhat on the northwest—a large granary, a horse

barn, and a cow barn lie in that direction—and directly north is a large, low building for machinery. The house is a story-and-a-half high, with a long lean-to on the north side, making a kitchen and pantry. The buildings are all painted red with white trimmings. They constitute quite a respectable outfit for a Dakota farm.

August 6, 1886
A beautiful day. The men are all harvesting. Not even a chore man is left on the place. They have been cutting sixty acres a day with all five harvesters running. Some of the men are shocking, and Walter is tagging after them with the horse and buggy. The reapers are flying all about us, stretching out their long white arms and grasping in the grain. They remind me of sea gulls as they glisten in the sunshine. The shocks which begin to dot the prairie look very beautiful as one passes miles of them standing in neat, straight rows— avenues of wheat-lined fields for miles and miles.

Washburn A Mill Explosion

The grinding of wheat into flour inevitably creates a fine dust that fills the air of a factory and coats the machinery within. The middlings purifier allowed millers to produce flour on an unprecedented scale, but the process created much more dust than millstones ever had. In the early years of Minneapolis's flour industry, few realized how easily this dust could be ignited. It took just one explosive event to trigger a flurry of innovations that would reduce the trade's dangers. On May 2, 1878, the Washburn A mill, touted as the "finest flouring mill in the world," exploded, killing eighteen workers and threatening the entire mill district. Debris rained down upon the city and flames swept through nearby buildings. One-third of Minneapolis's milling capacity was destroyed, as well as lumberyards, planing mills, a machine shop, a wheat-storage elevator, a railroad roundhouse, and numerous nearby residences. A month later, the ruins were still smoking, but by the end of the year seventeen mills, including some that had been completely rebuilt, were again in operation, the resilience of Minneapolis as a milling power undaunted.

~~~~~

Minneapolis attorney and pioneer schoolteacher **Edward E. Witchie** recalled the explosion in the 1877 speech excerpted here.

> A black and terrible cloud shot up into the sky. Three hundred feet it rose, loaded with huge rock, timbers and debris, three hundred feet the lurid and awful flames followed it. The sheet of flame seemed to cover the entire milling district. It seemed as if the fiery elements confined in the bowels of the earth had rushed forth and had sworn the destruction, at one blow, of fair Minneapolis.
>
> The scene was one of awful and sublime magnificence. For a moment I was spellbound and doubted the credibility of my senses. But scarcely had I time for doubt or astonishment when a terrific thunder struck that hill at its very base. In a moment the electro alarms called out the fire department, bells were pealing forth their wild and weird notes from their discordant throats, steam whistles shrilled in dire confusion. As soon as I recovered from the first shock, down the hill I bounded,

jumped on the hind end of a wagon already under full headway. When I reached the scene of fire and death, the raging flames had already spread wide and breathed hot from this fierce and lurid furnace of destruction. The great Washburn mill with solid stone walls six feet thick for some height was all blown to pieces. Two other of the finest mills in the state were demolished at the same time and in the same way. Six of the largest mills on the falls and the big elevator were now wrapped in flames. Two planing mills, two machine shops, a lumberyard and numerous cooperages soon added fuel to this mass of raging fire and, for a time, it seemed that the whole lower part of the city must be sacrificed to satisfy the greedy demand of the fire fiend. The fire department worked nobly, but they could do nothing against such fearful odds. . . . The shock was felt for miles; it even disturbed the waters of the Mississippi at St. Paul, ten miles distant. Pieces of stone, iron and debris were hurled all over the city and inflicted damage and some severe injuries.

A modified photograph showing the Washburn A mill blast, made from a view by William H. Jacoby, who had documented the west side milling district just days before the explosion dramatically altered the scene.

~~~~~

Mary Christian was the wife of John Augustus "Gus" Christian, whose company operated the Washburn A mill. She described the disaster in a letter to her sister, Carrie Hall, who served as lady assistant steward for their uncle Oliver Kelly's grange organization.

Minneapolis, Minn.
May 26, 1878

. . . The explosion was indeed a dreadful thing and we cannot feel thankful enough that Gus and Lou were not there at the time. You have no idea or can imagine what a complete wreck the mill was in two minutes time, of that huge building there was not one stone left upon another, Besides the large mill there were five other flour mills burned and Alberts storehouse but not any of his shops. The storehouse was filled with hoop poles. He lost about $1,500 but losing his business is what has hurt him most. If the boys get their insurance they will lose only about $10,000 to $15,000 apiece which they could stand without feeling it very much had they not lost their business. They have not decided what they will do yet about going into business again. Gov. Washburn is very anxious they should take the new mill. They had seven offers to go into business in three days after the explosion. Two were offers by telegram from large firms in the East. That shows people have confidence in them does it not? They had telegrams of sympathy from all parts of the United States and some from Europe.

When the explosion took place we were all at the tea table Emma and Pam were with us. We felt something jar the house it seemed. Gus and I had not risen from our chairs when the second jar came throwing open the sitting room door we then jumped to our feet Gus moving up stairs and I out doors. Mother thought it was an earthquake, but as soon as I reached the front of the house I saw an emensce column of smoke and flame it seemed directly behind the schoolhouse in front of our house. Gus took his hat and ran down town expecting every moment to come upon it and did not know it was his mill until he was within three blocks of it. He had heard before it was the City gasworks and so did not feel anxious. There was eighteen lives lost altogether but had it happened in the day time there could not have been less than two hundred (200) lost for in the big mill alone they employed forty men, Gus + Lou had been from the mill only one half hour it was rather a loud call for them was it not?

. . . I forgot to say that when the mill exploded nearly all the glass in the windows on Washington Ave. and some on Nicolet Ave were broken, it was reported that there was $10.00 worth of glass broken and there was an iron door in the bank

which was bolted thrown open. Pieces of wood and paper were found in St. Paul and the jar was felt in Stillwater. Two men were in a boat at St. Paul and the water was so much agitated it came up and filled up their boat so that they were obliged to go to shore. All the bodies have been found except three they do not think they will ever be found now.

Some railroad companies offered sightseeing trips, bringing tourists to the site just days after the explosion, where they could see the ruins still smoking from the blast that took eighteen lives and destroyed numerous businesses. ("The Minneapolis Calamity," *Harper's Weekly Magazine*, from a photograph by C. A. Zimmerman)

~~~~~

Stephen F. Peckham was professor of chemistry and physics at the University of Minnesota from 1874 to 1880. During this period he also served as chemist of the state geological survey and as state assayer. Among his numerous published reports on technical and scientific matters was the 1908 account titled *The Dust Explosions at Minneapolis May 2, 1878, and Other Dust Explosions.*

As I was sitting at the tea-table on the evening of May 2, 1878, I was startled by a noise as if a barrel of flour had been tipped over on the floor above. In a moment the sound was repeated. We all rushed to the door from which could be seen the flouring mills of the city, about a mile distant. A column of black smoke arose to a great height above the spot where the largest mill and an elevator had stood, and spreading out like an immense mushroom, it floated off with the wind, which was blowing from the large Washburn A mill towards the Diamond and Humboldt mills, they being directly behind the elevator from where I stood. The elevator, 108 feet high, was wrapped in flames from sill to ridge pole; if it had been drenched with oil it could not have ignited more quickly. Immediately after, flames were pouring from every window in the three mills to windward, standing on the banks of the river, which were wholly consumed but did not explode. . . .

The evidence shows conclusively that the explosion commenced in the Washburn mill. . . . there was a smouldering fire in the dust house, or the spouts leading to the dust house, in all probability the latter. There is but one way in which it is barely possible for a fire to originate in such a locality, and that is by sparks from the stones igniting little masses of loose dust, the latter being fanned into a blaze by the air draft. This blaze probably ignited all the dust in the spout and flour-dust house, which increased the pressure enough to burst the house and knock out the end of the spout . . . This was followed by the explosion of all the dust in the grinding-room, which had been thrown into the air by the bursting of the flour-dust house . . .

The outward impulse was produced by the expansion of the hot gases formed first by loose dust in the mill, but as these rose into the air, tending to form a vacuum below, the air from all direction rushed in, acting upon the flour, middlings, etc., that was in bulk, throwing it in all directions and adding to the power of the explosion. Probably, when the roof was a hundred feet high and the walls in all direction ten feet, the force of the explosion was much greater than at first. . . .

Though by far the most famous, the Washburn A was just one of many mills that exploded during this period. Science soon explained the volatility of flour dust, and the USDA Chemistry Department offered advice to millers.

Bigger and Better Flour Mills

The explosion of the Washburn A mill was the direct result of increased milling capacity and the accompanying dust produced by the machinery. Minneapolis millers turned catastrophe into opportunity as they rebuilt the leveled district with progressive mills equipped with the newest technology. One essential component soon in use industry-wide was a dust collector—the Behrns Millstone Exhaust—first installed in the Washburn mill by William de la Barre.

~~~~~~

The dominant structure on the east side of the river was the seven-story Pillsbury A mill. Built in 1880–81 by C. A. Pillsbury and Company, it was designed by architect LeRoy S. Buffington, who met the company's demands that the building be not only functional but

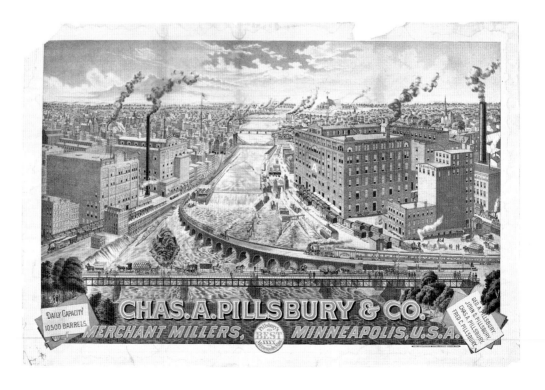

The Washburn-Crosby and Pillsbury Companies were engaged in fierce competition throughout much of their existence. Advertisements of one company's presence on the riverfront often neglected to display the buildings of its competitor. The Washburn-Crosby flour mill complex advertised in the *Northwestern Miller* in 1893 (above) incorrectly shows the A mill extending to the river, while the Charles A. Pillsbury and Company's 1885 view of the mill district (facing page) includes an out-of-proportion A mill, at the time the largest mill in the world.

also beautiful. Its daily flour milling capacity was four thousand barrels, and in the coming years improvements would make it the world's largest flour mill. The *Minneapolis Tribune* described "The Big Mill" on November 7, 1885.

> The building is 100 x 138 feet on the ground, with stone walls six feet thick at the base and eighteen inches on the top, and is seven and one-half stories high, including the cupola. . . . Entering on the ground floor we don a rubber coat and hat, and with a lantern in hand follow our guide, and descend by a narrow, steep flight of stairs 45 feet below, where the water wheels are, in the sub-basement. . . . In each side of this sub-basement is a Boyden Turbine water wheel, five feet in diameter. The two flumes through which the water is conducted from the race above, to the water wheels below, are each 40 feet long, six feet in diameter, and are made of cast and wrought iron riveted together in sections, and are also in the sub-basement. The

tunnels which conduct the water from the wheels are 13 feet wide and 16 feet deep, dug out through the sand rock and walled up with stone and brick laid in cement mortar. They come together and carry the water out to the river again, passing under the race. Returning to the first floor you see nothing but upright and horizontal shafts, wheels, pulleys and great heavy thick belts, which run the machinery all through the mills. One side is only a duplicate of the other, and the machinery stands so close together that there is scarcely room for a man to pass around through it. . . .

[T]his is not only the largest mill in America: it has no equal in the world in the perfection of its arrangement and completeness of its machinery. Neither pains nor expense have been spared, in supplying facilities which would, in the least degree, be beneficial in manufacturing superior flour.

C. A. Pillsbury and Company was formed in 1871 by **Charles A. Pillsbury** with his brother John A. Pillsbury and his uncle J. S. Pillsbury. By 1882, the Pillsbury A flour mill—with a capacity of 5,107 barrels per day—was the largest in the world. Charles was a mechanical innovator—his mill was the first to use electrical lighting—and savvy businessman who sought to broaden the market for his products, which by 1897 included ready-to-cook breakfast cereals.

Washburn, Crosby and Company was formed in 1879 by **Cadwallader C. Washburn** and John Crosby, along with George H. Christian and W. H. Dunwoody, and its mills were soon producing ten thousand barrels of flour per day. In 1880, the company swept the prizes at the Millers' National Association's first and only exhibition. Based on these accolades, the company advertised its product as "Gold Medal Flour," a brand that soon became world famous.

Journalist and author **Eugene V. Smalley** wrote for a number of eastern magazines and publications. In 1882 he traveled west from Lake Superior to report on the northwestern states and territories for *Century Magazine*. He later established the *Northwest Illustrated Monthly Magazine*, which covered the resources of the region served by the Northern Pacific Railroad. He settled permanently in St. Paul in 1884. His 1886 article "The Flour-Mills of Minneapolis" is excerpted here.

A great flouring-mill is a wonderful aggregation of delicate and ingenious mechanical processes. The manner in which the wheat, middlings, and flour circulate

Charles A. Pillsbury (left) was described as "one of the greatest millers of all time." Cadwallader C. Washburn (right) intended the Washburn A mill to be "the finest flouring mill in the world" and soon claimed that it made "such flour as was never before seen on this continent."

through the eight or nine stories, from side to side, from floor to floor, from machine to machine, nowhere needing the help of human hands, makes it seem like one vast living organism. . . . From the time the grain comes into the mill in cars to the packing up of the fine flour in barrels, through all the processes of sifting, cleaning, grinding, purifying, separating, etc., everything is automatic. No workman touches the product save in the way of supervision. Indeed, the laborers stand related to the machines about as the policemen do to the moving crowd in Broadway. They see that order is preserved and the movement is not clogged. The wide apartments of the mill, crowded with machines ranged in regular lines, seem deserted as the visitor roams through them. Perhaps in a distant corner a man may be perceived, slowly moving about, looking phantom-like in his white garments, seen through a mist of flour-dust. He is an assistant miller, who perhaps has a hundred roller mills in his charge, all briskly grinding away from morning to night. There is no racket or clatter amid these serried rows of apparatus. The whole great building hums and pulsates with a dull, buzzing noise, but no particular piece of enginery seems to give out a special note. As the sounds of a great city mingle in a subdued roar, so do the thousand voices of the mill unite to produce a single continuous effect on the ear. . . .

And for favorable conditions for grinding wheat no place in the world can compare with Minneapolis, if success is the measure of natural advantages. It is on the highways of rail transportation which lead from the grain-fields of the North-west to the great cities and sea-ports of the East. Nature turns its hundreds of wheels with an unfailing water-power, the climate is healthful and invigorating, and finally, it possesses an enterprising, intelligent, inventive population, made up of excellent elements drawn from the Eastern States, and broadened and energized by the opportunities and liberalism of Western business life. Its people believe enthusiastically in their city, and work together heartily to further its interests.

"Perhaps in a distant corner a man may be perceived" in the Washburn A mill in 1875. Though the flour mills were Minneapolis's largest industry, very few workers were actually required to run the machines. (William H. Jacoby, photos)

The Millers, Packers, and Sweepers

L ike many large industries, flour milling was prone to occasional labor strife. The first flour millers' strike occurred in 1879 to oppose planned wage reductions. Unions worked hard to organize from 1895 to 1900, and in 1902 they suggested that the Minneapolis mill companies lead the industry by guaranteeing millers an eight-hour day, a policy long advocated by the union. While skilled workers were successful in their campaign, their unskilled coworkers received different treatment. When in 1903 the flour loaders, too, demanded an eight-hour day and the union sought increased pay for women packers, management balked at these potential costs, brought in strikebreakers, and ultimately destroyed the union. Nearly fifteen years later, in 1917, Washburn-Crosby packers used a strike to pressure management for higher wages and, because the country was at war and immediate action was required, the strike was successful and unionism was revived. This triumph lasted only a short time in the decidedly anti-union city: management in some mills hired private investigators to undermine the unions by ferreting out organizers, who were summarily fired. As the International Union of Flour and Cereal Mill Employees fought to establish a workers' union to replace the company union, management spread anti-union propaganda. By 1921, the union was in tatters, permitted to exist with the promise to mill owners that the "half-hearted" organization would not harm the industry.

~~~~~~

Lifelong labor organizer **Jean E. Spielman** worked for both the Industrial Workers of the World and the American Federation of Labor. While organizing Northwestern flour mills from 1918 to 1921—including those in closed-shop Minneapolis, where business owners frowned upon unions that were not company-run—he printed the labor treatise *The Intricacies of the Wheat Pit*, which decried the long hours and low wages endured by flour mill employees.

The Workers' Share in the Profits
It is a sad commentary upon civilization that an industry flourishing to the extent as the flour milling industry is, that the workers employed in that industry are the

most under-paid next to the steel industry. The twelve-hour a day is still a fact in many a flour mill in the United States, and that the men are not satisfied with conditions in existence in the flour mills is bourne out by the fact that the mill owners are unable to keep their crews at work. Under the pretext of "more production," mill workers in some of the mills in Minnesota were compelled to work a long stretch of sixteen hours, men are quitting their jobs daily to seek other more remunerative employment; in fact, the turn over of labor in the milling industry has its parallel in the lumber industry; one crew leaving one crew at work, and another crew on the way coming to work, only to repeat the vicious process again and again.

. . . The mill owners in Minneapolis, as elsewhere, never advanced wages on account of the high cost of living, but the raise in wages came as a result of the organized efforts of the workers in the mills; the mill owners heard the rumblings, the pressure was too great, and they unloosened the purse strings. The conveyor

Workers bag flour in the Pillsbury A mill, 1902, the same year they negotiated an eight-hour workday and a six-day workweek. "Pillsbury's Best" brand was meant to describe the flour's superior quality, but it also served as an answer to the Washburn-Crosby ad campaign: "Eventually: Why Not Now?" Well, because "Pillsbury's Best."

dropped a few grains into the workers' pantry, and furthermore, the mill workers are not receiving higher pay than "similar semi-skilled or unskilled labor in any other industry" . . . The building laborer and hod carrier is receiving from 10 to 15 cents per hour more than the sweeper, roustabout, loader, trucker, oiler and in some places more than the packer, also than the grinder, and the building laborer is out in the open—breathing fresh air. Unlike the mill worker, who is inhaling the dust and has to submit to a "Simon Legree" type of a foreman imposing the 12-hour task, and in some unorganized mills, a double header of 16 hours; regular old fashion Union hours. Eight hours in the morning and eight hours in the afternoon.

William C. Edgar was born in La Crosse, Wisconsin, and settled in Minneapolis in 1882. Beginning in 1886 he served as the editor of the *Northwestern Miller*, a trade journal with a worldwide circulation. In 1892 his article "The Miller and His Mill" was published in *The Chautauquan.*

William C. Edgar, editor of the *North-western Miller*, also organized an 1891 relief movement for famine sufferers in Russia and chaired a committee that sent thirty-five carloads of flour to the needy of San Francisco after the 1906 earthquake.

The miller of the present is a manufacturer of flour and a dweller in cities. Frequently he has but a slight technical knowledge of his trade and spends more time on 'Change than in his mill proper. He is a man of affairs and has to do with foreign exchange. He draws his information not in the old simple manner from direct, personal contact and gossip with his neighbors over his halfdoor, but from cables and telegrams and a wide range of correspondents located in many lands far and near. He studies international and not neighborhood conditions and disposes of his product not on the toll and exchange principle, but through an army of agents. His mill is not a placid, murmuring, poetic, and artistic ivy-grown structure, lurking modestly on some quiet stream half hidden by trees, but a huge and, alas too often, a hideous looking factory, puffing and pounding and trembling away day and night in an effort to turn out all the flour it can, driven by mighty engines, or powerful turbines, or both. The wheat does not come to it direct from farmers' wagons, unloaded by horny-handed agriculturists, prone to drive a sharp bargain and exchange gossip, but by long train loads, over switches built for the purpose from the main line to the mill. To pay for the constant stream of wheat which comes into his mill and to find a market for the barrels and sacks of flour which pour out of it, taxes the brain of to-day's miller to the utmost, and forces him—harassed as he is by the manipulations of his raw material, by the grain gamblers—to exert all his energy and business ability to keep his huge

Grain storage of the future: Frank H. Peavey, an active member of a Minneapolis grain company and owner of numerous Midwestern elevators, brainstormed on the storage issue in 1899 with Charles F. Haglin, an architect and building contractor. Peavey and Haglin saw the merits of concrete over wood as a building material. Though skeptics believed that pressure would cause a concrete structure to crack when the contents were drawn out, the pair soon proved them wrong. In 1899 they collaborated to build the world's first cylindrical solid concrete grain elevator. After testing it they found that the structure was not weakened by the pressure of its contents, nor was the grain spoiled. Peavey and Haglin soon designed and built in Duluth a multiple-tower concrete elevator with a million-bushel capacity, and the grain storage industry would never be the same.

machine moving and still come out whole at the end of the year. The complete change which has occurred in the character of the miller and his plant may be said to date from the beginning of the "new process" in milling, which began to be inaugurated in the United States about twenty years ago.

. . . when the new process was introduced, Minneapolis, with her fine water power and her already thriving group of mills, with her developing resources and her fortunate location near the wheat fields of the northwest, above all, with her few but highly intelligent, progressive, and daring millers, stood in a most advantageous position to profit by it and did so to such an extent that four mills of a size which would appear impossible to millers of a previous era, were speedily erected. Minneapolis soon assumed a position as the largest flour producing city in the United States, quickly achieving the pre-eminence she now holds as the milling center of the world, having an actual capacity of over 43,000 barrels per day.

～～～～～

In 2001, the Minnesota Historical Society interviewed mill workers employed by the Pills-bury and Washburn-Crosby Companies from the 1940s to the 1990s. Although their recollections are of an industry past its prime at the falls, the tasks they describe differ little from those done there in the 1910s and 1920s, and they offer an insider's perspective on the workings of a flour mill.

～～～～～

John "Pat" Patricelli worked in the Pillsbury mill beginning in 1961 and held several positions, among them loader, packer, and millwright.

I started out at Pillsbury as a loader. The loader's job was to load the sacks of flour in the boxcars. We had a two-man crew in which we had to work together loading

"The best looking crew that ever worked in the mills." Washburn-Crosby packers of the 1920s pose for the company photographer. (*Eventually News*)

the boxcars. The flour bags came down the chute on to a spring conveyor belt into the boxcar. One person would take one sack and put it into place, then the other would take the next sack and put it into place. When we had a high load, like eight feet high, the both of us would grab the sack and throw it into place. In the winter when loading the boxcars I can remember the wind and cold was so bad the warm bags of flour kept us warm. The coldest day I remember when working the wind chill was 72 degrees below zero.

Then I signed up for the Packing Department and became a packer. My first job was to work on the merry-go-round. This is what the company called it because I packed at one packer then went to the other packers. The products that were packed were the by-products from the mill such as wheat germ, rolled wheat, and other products that were not the flour. I had to continue packing to empty the small bins or the flour mill would have to shut down. This was very hard work because I had to pack everything by hand. I had to open the sack or bag and put it on a tube, then hold the sack closed so the product would not blow out of the bag. I put my foot on the foot pedal which engaged the belt to start the packer. The sack would fill up to the weighted amount, then I picked up the sack or bag and put it onto the scale and filled it by a hand scoop to get to the right weight. Then I sewed the sack or bag with a sewing machine. Most of the sacks or bags were 100 pounds and sometimes 140 pounds.

Workers fill and seal bags at Russell-Miller Milling Company in Minneapolis, 1924. (Charles J. Hibbard, photo)

Louis J. Hornicek worked for the Washburn-Crosby Company as a packer and a loader beginning in 1941.

> *Sometimes we'd get an order for maybe a thousand sacks. The whole thousand would go in one boxcar. As they were packing, it would come through some chutes right into the boxcar. Maybe there would be four of us. It would come on a table and you had to put in on the truck and set it in. After it would get higher, you'd have to put it on your back and throw it up. A thousand sacks took a lot of space. . . You'd get flour around your head as you put them on your shoulder. You'd go home with flour around your ears and neck and so forth.*

Don Hinrichs worked for the Washburn-Crosby Company beginning in 1944, filling boxcars, packing and loading flour, and running steam engines.

> It was a lot of bull work, to tell you the truth. Anything in the flourmills was a lot of bull work, heavy work, I mean. You had to be in pretty good shape to do it. Like, up on the packing floor when I was up there, I was pretty good size so some of the milling stuff comes in 120- and 140-pound bags. They'd come into the boxcar to the table off of the conveyor belts and you'd have to take them to the end of the boxcar and load them in there. With 120- and 140-pounds, you'd keep pretty busy. The sacks would keep coming and coming. It's like Lucy with the chocolates. They don't stop. They just keep coming. If you don't get back quick enough, they go on the floor and it was harder to pick them up off the floor. You have to put them on your shoulder, and, sometimes, you'd have to hoist them up. You know how big boxcars are.
>
> . . .when you loaded boxcars, the boxcars were out on the track. You're inside and you pick up a load of flour on a little two-wheel truck and then you'd have to go outside with it in the boxcar and then you'd come back in and get another load. That's all you did all day long.

Dorothy McLinn began working for the Washburn-Crosby Company during World War II as a sweeper, filling a position traditionally held by men. From 1945 to 1959 she was a member of the personnel department.

"Such beautiful clothes." Women packed flour on the Washburn-Crosby mill's fifth floor, which was nicknamed "no man's land." (*Eventually News*)

Packing flour in the Pillsbury mills, 1939. (Courtesy Library of Congress)

Sometimes the machines would clog and dust would fly. . . That's why we wore those beautiful clothes. We had to have our hair covered. . . . It was kind of monotonous. It's like cleaning a house. You could do it every day, dust every day, and that's what we did because there was dust.

~~~~~~~

Sheridan Granger worked for the Washburn-Crosby Company in a variety of positions, from sweeper to second miller, beginning in 1940.

As a sweeper, I swept on the deck of the C-Mill. The machinery that is up there, the dust collector. . . Sometimes, I thought it was futile because the dust collectors, as I was sweeping, the dust was coming right out. But my boss would say, "It's never the same dust."

PACKAGING THE FLOUR

Flour had traditionally been packed in barrels, and a cooperage industry grew up around the falls, beginning with the J. B. Bassett Company, established in 1859. The Hall and Dann Barrel Company in the 1880s was the world's largest cooperage, employing 175 workers and producing six thousand barrels each day. In 1901, the peak year, 3,451,000 barrels were manufactured. That figure tells only part of the tale, however: by that year only 20 percent of the flour manufactured at the falls was shipped in those barrels. Cloth and paper bags were becoming a more popular means of shipping flour, and by 1915 the Hall and Dann Barrel Company became the Northern Bag Company.

Skilled workers at a cooperage pose with tools and products of the trade in 1902. A significant labor innovation in the local industry dated to 1874: cooperative barrel factories, owned and operated by the workers themselves, set up networks to ensure steady work and preserve their craft. (John Runk, photo)

From the *Northwestern Miller*, November 1, 1878.

A spectator cannot but be entertained by the busy sight presented in the factory. It is a building 140 feet long, in which twenty seven active coopers keep time with a lively whacking of hammers, interspersed now and then with a joke or a good natured remark "on the fly," for they work by the piece and each man is bent on showing a good record for his time. Besides the coopers there are about ten men and boys employed about the engine and machinery. The building is heated by steam and is very convenient and comfortable. With the entire force the shop turns out five hundred barrels a day, and still the orders from the mills tax the factory to keep a sufficient supply ready. A trial of speed was made by the coopers the other day, which resulted in making fifty-six barrels in an hour. That was lively work. Coopers' wages at present are nine cents for ten-hoop barrels and ten cents for twelve-hoop barrels, and one very satisfactory feature of their employment is that they have steady work summer and winter, with prompt pay in cash.

Joseph W. Tyra was an office worker and a salesman for International Multifoods Corporation in New Prague beginning in 1906. In an oral history interview recorded in 1958, he described work in a cooperage.

We had a cooper shop [at the mill] where they used to make an average of four or five hundred wooden barrels a day. . . . when I first started there I remember coopers receiving seven cents for each barrel they put together . . . A good man averaged around thirty barrels a day, he would make a couple dollars a day which in seven days was good pay. Then later on some of those fellows would get to be experts, I've heard of some of these men making as high as fifty barrels a day.

. . . all the staves, hoops that were bought came there in carloads . . . They came flat and each cooper had

his little round stove . . . and they would have a fire in the stove and by putting these staves around that they would sort of heat up and enable the cooper to bring them in the shape of a barrel, see. . . . It was certain moisture in those staves that enabled [the cooper] to bend it without breaking the staves. Very seldom that they ever broke a stave. Those barrels when they were put together they really held flour in good shape. There was no paper container inside or anything. There were air tight. . . . in later years I think they started to put paper inside, but originally there was just the wooden barrel . . . The cooper shop disappeared when the baker started to buy flour in burlaps and cotton sacks. Of course, one of the reasons for the barrel disappearing too was those bakers in New York and Philadelphia used to fire the ovens with the staves from the barrels and then when they got gas ovens and electric ovens they had no use for the barrels to burn in their ovens.

From the *Northwestern Miller*, February 22, 1884.

"What is the coming package for flour?" . . . "Is the bag growing in favor?"

It is, for a fact. We have for some time been selling bagged flour in some parts of New England and the demand for it is gradually increasing. The greatest objection to it in this country is that the fuzz wears off the burlaps and of course gets into the flour. Now it is a well known fact that all flour should be sifted before using, and the sieve catches every bit of this fuzz, which is as clean as splinters from barrel wood. To remove this objection we have tried putting cotton sacks inside the burlaps, and this was perfectly satisfactory to consumers, but the cost is equal to barreling, and the great argument now in favor of the sack is its cheapness. A heavy cotton sack is now being made by Bemis, Bro. & Co., of this city, which seems to meet all objections and is clean. It is fast growing in favor east, and may yet take the place of the barrel. The cost is about the same as the burlap, and the color is a cross between the com-

mon cotton and the jute sack, the heavy cottons being unbleached. Europe uses sacks for everything sackable, and there is no complaint there about burlap fuzz. The burlap bag makers are trying to devise a process for so finishing the burlap as to wholly prevent the fuzz from rubbing loose and mingling with the flour. If they are successful in this, there will be little opposition to the general introduction of the burlap as a flour package, and it will then come from flour and warehousemen at seaports and elsewhere. In New York, for instance, any old shell of a building is considered good enough to store flour in. I have seen flour stored in buildings along with broom corn and other stuff which makes good rat nests, the floors being littered up with all sorts of refuse. When we get fine stone and cement storehouses for flour, like those of the old country, the burlap will be quite as safe a package as the barrel.

By the 1880s bags were replacing barrels for the transport of flour. According to the *Northwestern Miller,* "The very many advantages of bags over barrels in handling of flour, their cheapness, utility and convenience and economy in storing when empty are well known and the demand for bags for this and similar usages is rapidly increasing." Bemis, Brother & Co., a St. Louis firm, established a bag factory in Minneapolis in 1881 with a capacity of 75,000 bags per day.

From the *Northwestern Miller,* April 22, 1892.
A Big Bag Factory
Of the numerous manufactories possessed by Minneapolis, she is prouder of none than of the Bemis Bro. Bag Co.'s plant. Closely allied with the mills, this factory has come to be considered as almost one of them in interests. Starting out in a modest way in 1880, the Minneapolis factory of the company has kept pace with the growth and development of milling in the northwest, until it has expanded into a very large and important institution. . . . This building . . . is one of the most commanding and prominent in the southern part of the city. Its large size and bold lines of exterior give it a rich and massive aspect, and the appearance of the exterior is well supplemented by the fine interior construction. In dimensions on the ground, 66x150 feet, the structure has seven stories, besides basement. The front is of red pressed brick, and the rest of the walls of yellow brick. Everything about the building is very heavy and substantial, and the details throughout impress one as being designed for hard, every-day service, rather than for unnecessary show.

The building was planned and arranged with the single purpose in view of affording the Bemis company every facility and convenience for carrying on its business in the most economical and expeditious manner, and that this object is eminently attained will be promptly conceded by all who visit the factory. In fitting up the building, every possible feature has been introduced that could facilitate the making of bags or in any way contribute to the health and convenience of those employed within its walls. The various stories are high, airy and well lighted, and the floors are supported by 15 inch oak timbers.

Over 100 hands are regularly employed. The company is firmly wedded to the belief that money expended in liberally compensating employees is well invested, and to the credit of this company can it be said that few other concerns pay their help so generously.

Facing page: "No sight in a General Mills plant is more interesting than the packing crews. One girl fills the sack, another weighs, and a third sews. The speed they attain is amazing," noted a 1940 General Mills publication. Women generally packed the smaller five- and ten-pound bags of flour. (Bruce Sifford Studio, photo)

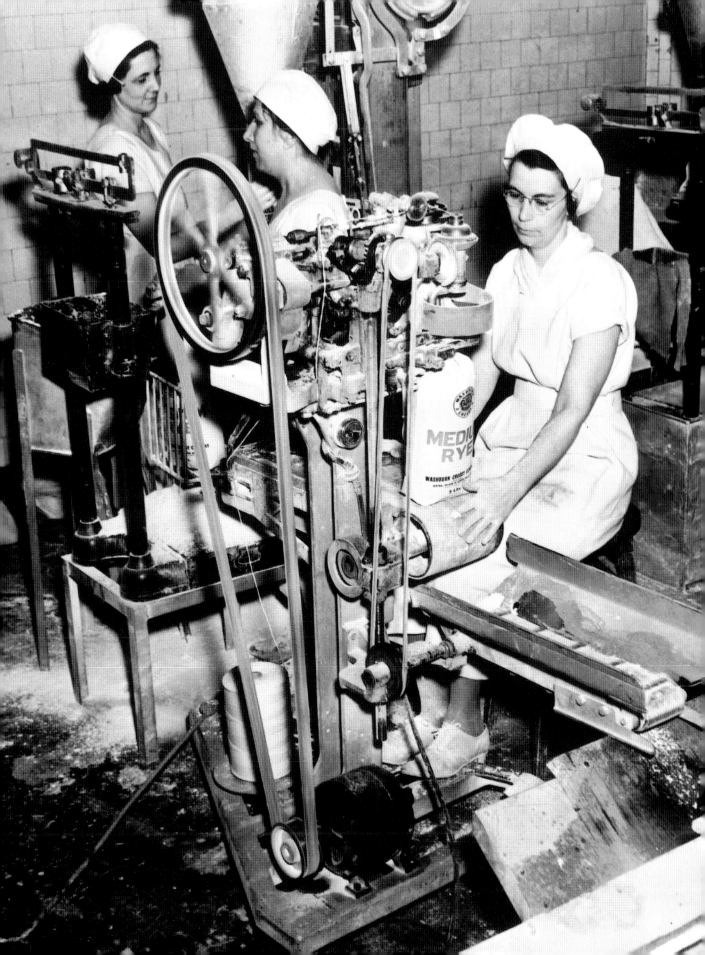

Flour Milling Giants

Minneapolis flour milling production peaked from 1909 to 1920, when the mills on average shipped sixteen million barrels annually. The Mill City reached its zenith in 1915–16, with twenty million barrels. After that year, however, Minneapolis's reign over the flour milling industry declined, the result of waning quality and quantity of spring wheat, changes in distribution patterns, and a tariff that benefited Buffalo, New York, more than Minneapolis. In 1930 Buffalo became the nation's flour milling center, removing Minneapolis from the cherished spot it had held for fifty years. The Washburn A shut down in 1965 and Pillsbury mills significantly reduced production over the course of the following decades as the companies shifted from flour milling to food processing for a global market.

During the flour mills' heyday early in the century, the largest companies at the falls were those whose names remain recognizable today: Pillsbury and General Mills. Both companies built on their flour milling success by diversifying and reaching out to consumers. Pillsbury focused on promotion to individuals through recipes tested in its modern kitchen, packaged convenience foods and cake and dough mixes, and radio advertisements by its Pillsbury Dough Boys orchestra. In 1949 the popular Pillsbury Bake-Off was launched, and amateur cooks continue to compete with recipes using "Pillsbury's Best" flour.

In 1928, James Ford Bell of Washburn-Crosby oversaw the incorporation of General Mills, which included companies headquartered in California, Texas, and Michigan, in order to eliminate wasteful overlaps in mills, grain storage, and merchandising products. In this new incarnation, General Mills created Wheaties, Bisquick, and other popular products, developed the radio station WCCO to expand its advertising, and christened Betty Crocker as a link between flour producers and the average housewife. Though no longer anchored at the falls, the company remains a Minnesota icon, headquartered in Golden Valley. After acquiring former rival Pillsbury Foods in 2001, General Mills distributes many familiar brands, including Hamburger Helper, Pillsbury dough products, Betty Crocker desserts, and Green Giant vegetables.

Betty Crocker was a character developed by General Mills in response to letters from housewives seeking culinary advice. She still represents domestic comfort and harmony— a maternal figure who knows how to entertain and dispenses advice with a flourish.

A host of advertising and baking specialists promoted the Betty persona, and she provided boxed cake mixes, kitchen-tested recipes, radio broadcasts on homemaking advice, and a published column answering questions from the family cook—including counsel on wholesome menus and economical shopping. Her character was so carefully cultivated that she was once voted the second-best-known-woman in America (after Eleanor Roosevelt).

A Betty Crocker radio show broadcast in July 1930 is excerpted here.

"America's favorite homemaker": Betty Crocker, ca. 1930.

Hello, radio friends.

There's no trick at all any more to making that favorite summertime dessert of American men, Fresh Cherry Cobbler. Not since Bisquick has appeared on the market! And not only can you make it in a miraculously short time with ever so little work. But you will have a Fresh Cherry Cobbler that your husband will say is by far the best Cherry Cobbler he has ever tasted! One that will endear you to him forever!

. . . The combination of flavors in Bisquick Fresh Cherry Cobbler, rich and refreshing, is really too good to describe. And it is a handsome as well as a delicious dessert! Rare beauty lies in its lovely blend of colors. The snowy white of the rich Bisquick foundation . . . so feathery light and fluffy! The delicate golden brown of the tender crust! The sparkling red of the cherries! The gleaming ruby sauce! And on top of it all, if you like, a drift of whipped cream.

The recipe for Fresh Cherry Cobbler is another one of the modernized speed recipes for dishes with old-fashioned charm contained in the new book, "101 Bisquick Recipes." Send a Bisquick box top for your copy today. It will be a valuable and inspiring addition to your kitchen library . . . supplying you with suggestions for bringing additional joy to your husband 365 days a year!

Reclaiming

THE RIVERFRONT

A New Identity

St. Anthony Falls took on its role as a hardworking waterpower when the government mill began producing lumber in 1822. A century later, as flour milling companies moved their operations east—particularly to Buffalo, New York—and west in order to take advantage of lower shipping rates, the falls and riverfront fell into disuse. From 1930 until about 1970, the riverfront's popularity ebbed to its lowest point: no longer a bustling industrial site, its significance as the city's birthplace was forgotten. However, by the 1980s, local agencies and individuals began to focus on adaptive reuse of historic buildings, the beauty of the river and falls, and the history of the district. Their actions helped to reclaim the riverfront as an integral part of the city.

~~~~~

After 1930, most of the flour mills shut down one by one, and the once lively riverfront district gradually deteriorated. Many buildings were simply vacated, some, including the west side row along the river, were demolished. The west side canal was sealed, railroad trestles along it razed, and, later, the mill ruins filled in with gravel. Soon only the Washburn A on the west side and the Pillsbury A on the east side continued producing flour, and then in 1965 the Washburn A ceased operations when General Mills moved its headquarters to Golden Valley.

As the flour milling era came to an end, the possibilities of navigation on the upper river, a goal discussed periodically since the city's early rivalries with St. Paul, once again came to the fore. Residents of Minneapolis had long lamented that the drop at the Falls of St. Anthony—much as it benefited Minneapolis industries—had prevented boat traffic from reaching the upper river. The Rivers and Harbors Act approved by the U.S. Congress in 1937 dictated the dredging of a nine-foot channel to facilitate transportation, making way for the Upper Minneapolis Harbor Project, which through two sets of locks brought boats into an extensive landing area some distance above the falls. Between 1950 and 1963, the Army Corps of Engineers installed the two locks, covered the falls with a permanent concrete apron, removed what was left of Spirit Island, and modified bridges, including the Stone Arch Bridge, replacing two of its sections with steel trusses. With these lock systems in place, Minneapolis was at last tied to national water transportation routes, and the area around the falls had once again been significantly altered.

The use of the falls' waterpower was also evolving, with hydroelectric plants becoming the primary consumers. Northern States Power took over the waterpower leases made available by the closing of the mills and the Twin City Rapid Transit Company's conversion from streetcars to buses, and by 1960 the falls that had powered so many lumber and flour mills generated electricity almost exclusively. The St. Anthony Falls Hydraulic Laboratory, an experiment station run by the University of Minnesota, also began to utilize a portion of the waterpower for its projects.

Despite these many changes, the district remained an industrial site: mill buildings were adapted to warehouse space, the locks gave barges access to the upper river, and NSP converted water to hydroelectricity for use in the region. However, dreams of the Upper Mississippi becoming a hardworking river, with countless barges using the harbor, were clearly overblown, and the district's identity began to shift. Other ideas about how the riverfront could be used for work and leisure began accumulating, and in the late 1960s, as buildings in the nearby Gateway district were torn down and replaced by parking lots, people began to seek alternatives to outright destruction of the old to make way for the new.

The Upper Lock, under construction here in 1960, opened the river to navigation above St. Anthony Falls. Visible at right is a concrete spillway built by the Army Corps of Engineers to permanently protect the falls. (Dale L. Sperline, photo)

National and local programs put into place in the 1970s inspired local agencies to focus on the riverfront's possibilities for adaptive reuse. When the St. Anthony Falls Historic District was named to the National Register of Historic Places in 1971, the buildings in the area were officially protected. In response to many proposals, a cornerstone plan titled "Mississippi/Minneapolis" was published in 1972, and numerous groups, including the City of Minneapolis, the Minneapolis Park and Recreation Board (MPRB), the Minneapolis Housing and Redevelopment Authority (MHRA), the Minneapolis Heritage Preservation Commission, and (later) the Minnesota Historical Society, took part in revitalizing the central riverfront. The MHRA (which later became the Minneapolis Community Development Agency) created formal redevelopment projects to be implemented along the river, and the MPRB prepared a comprehensive plan for a regional park

A skyline view of the west side from the St. Anthony Falls Hydraulic Laboratory shows the upper lock (right) and modifications to the Stone Arch Bridge to accommodate river traffic. Beyond the bridge and to the right of the concrete grain elevators is the Washburn A mill prior to the 1991 fire that nearly destroyed it. (Elizabeth M. Hall, photo)

encompassing the central riverfront. Additionally, in 1972, the Federal Water Pollution Control Act, which later became known as the Clean Water Act, began regulating pollutants dumped into U.S. waters, including the Mississippi River. This act encouraged localities nationwide to clean up their water and in Minneapolis altered the riverfront from a sewage repository to a potentially appealing destination.

Early projects along the west side demonstrated the value of the site and encouraged people to give the river a second look. Fuji-Ya, a Japanese restaurant opened by Reiko Weston in 1968, was built where the Basset lumber mill and Columbia flour mill once stood, and the First Street Station restaurant, opened by James Howe in 1975 in a former railroad engine house, was the first adaptive reuse of existing structures on the west side.

On the east side, more ambitious projects were undertaken. Peter Nelson Hall renovated an 1890s saloon into Pracna on Main restaurant, which opened in 1973. Louis Zelle launched St. Anthony Main, a restaurant, retail, entertainment, office, and residential complex, in the late 1970s. The pedestrian-friendly mall was converted from a mattress factory, ironworks, and other historic structures. Soon to follow was Riverplace, a residential, office, and retail space that opened opposite Nicollet Island in 1984.

During this period the Minneapolis riverfront—like others across the country—was being reintroduced as a destination for living, working, and shopping. The MPRB sought to make people aware of the river, creating public parkland along its banks and developing trails that made the river accessible for the first time in decades. Increased access and visibility made the river an amenity to be enjoyed. Acquisition of riverfront land near the falls for park purposes began on the east bank: the site of Father Hennepin Bluffs Park was acquired in 1977, followed quickly by Nicollet Island and Main Street in 1978, Boom Island in 1982, and the B. F. Nelson site in 1987. On the west bank, the park board acquired the West River Parkway corridor between 1985 and 1988 through a series of purchases from railroads, a gravel company, and a gas utility. The subsequent development of each of these parcels with green space, trails, parkways, and other amenities in turn encouraged additional private development of the adjacent land. The emphasis of many of these park projects has been on historical restoration and interpretation and, thanks to these acquisitions, virtually the entire riverfront from the south city limits through the northern edge of the milling district is in public ownership.

With the mixed success of the early private development projects and the catalyst of adjacent park amenities, numerous additional mills, warehouses, and commercial buildings were adapted to new uses, particulary residential, including in the 1980s the Whitney Hotel (previously the Standard Mill) and Mill Place (converted from warehouses) and a decade later North Star Lofts (previously the North Star Woolen Mills). The opportunity to work and play along the river was augmented by the option of living within view of St. Anthony Falls.

The development of Nicollet Island—with its emphasis on recreation and on the area's history—represented a further evolution of structure and land use at the riverfront. Home to a mix of industry, business, and residential buildings, Nicollet Island had long been envisioned as a park, and in the late 1970s and early 1980s urban green space was developed on the island's south side. The MPRB refurbished the historic William Bros Boiler Works as a public pavilion with adjacent picnic areas and decks offering views of the falls. Rather than remove the longstanding neighborhood on the north side of the island, the park board agreed to enter into an unusual nominal-fee land lease agreement with the owners of those structures, which actually stand on park property. Once home to the city's elite, this area now showcases historic nineteenth-century frame houses, some restored on site and some moved from other locations in the city. Luxury row houses built by William W. Eastman in the 1870s were also renovated as historic condominiums.

Further promotion of the history of the city's birthplace has been carried out by the St. Anthony Falls Heritage Board, created in 1988. Working with federal funding and

In 1948, the ruins of the west side mill district lay before the Washburn-Crosby concrete elevators and A mill, which would continue as the sole flour operation on the west side for nearly twenty years, closing in 1965.

matching funds from other groups, this interagency board supervised the opening of the Stone Arch Bridge to pedestrian traffic in 1994, attracting walkers, joggers, and bikers to the riverfront. Two years later the bridge became an important link in the St. Anthony Falls Heritage Trail, a self-guided tour to the area's geological, engineering, and industrial history through maps, kiosks, and trail markers.

Large-scale interpretation of the riverfront's history was undertaken through Mill Ruins Park and Mill City Museum. Excavation of the west side mill ruins began in 2000, and archaeologists uncovered walls of flour mills built in the 1860s and 1870s, the trestle supports for the Minneapolis Eastern Railroad, and a tailrace canal that once again carries water from the river to a location downstream from the falls. The MPRB completed the first phase of Mill Ruins Park in 2001, with additional phases to be implemented as funding becomes available.

The Minnesota Historical Society's

Seeking clues to the past: an archeological exploration of the west side mill ruins in 2000 revealed the district's tailraces and a wagon bridge that crossed them. The neon Gold Medal Flour sign, now restored atop the grain elevators, is visible at street level near the Washburn A mill ruins. (© 2000 Star Tribune/Minneapolis-St. Paul)

Mill City Museum opened in 2003 within the Washburn A mill, severely damaged by fire in 1991 but now stabilized. The museum exhibits recount the history of flour milling, the development of industries along the riverfront, and the expansion of railroads and agriculture. Visitors can explore baking and waterpower laboratories and experience an eight-story exhibit ride that simulates the powerful, noisy, industrial process of turning wheat into flour. An observation deck on the ninth and uppermost floor of the museum offers a bird's-eye view of the surrounding mill district, the falls, and the river.

With these developments and others, including the new Guthrie Theater, the evolving riverfront—home to industry, business, and leisure opportunities—now plays a central role in art, culture, and recreation in Minneapolis. Repeating an earlier phase of their history, the falls and river are once again prized destinations.

EPILOGUE

St. Anthony Falls has attracted people throughout history, from the Ojibwe who worshipped this area as a sacred site, to tourists who marveled at the "wild beauty of the rapids," to entrepreneurs who harnessed the waterpower to drive their sawmills and flour mills. As white settlement spread westward, the cataract proved an obvious site for a city, and Minneapolis's location at the crossroads of the region allowed for an influx of people and materials and the shipment of finished products both east and west. From 1848 to 1887, as the leading exporter of lumber cut from vast northern pineries, Minneapolis was the Sawdust Town. From 1880 to 1930, its mills turned out enough flour, ground from Minnesota and Dakota wheat, to be the nation's principal flour producer, the Mill City. Before these commercial successes, however, the falls area was a tourist stop, whether its viewers were explorers evaluating the region's plenty or East Coast travelers on a grand tour of the Northwest. Today the falls attract tourists once again; though the industries surrounding them have all but stopped, the waterfall remains, still a source of power and a means of transportation.

For a time, Minneapolis turned its back on its birthplace, but numerous symbols—the river, the falls, the Stone Arch Bridge, the Pillsbury A mill, and the Washburn A mill—still exist as reminders of what made the Mill City unique. As the riverfront is transformed into a lively residential district with tourist attractions and parks, increasing attention focuses squarely where it should: on the falls that started it all.

Today the mill district draws visitors for a host of activities, from watching boats pass through the lock and exploring Mill City Museum (left), to hiking the St. Anthony Falls Heritage Trail and wandering through the east side's parks and historic buildings (above). (John Lindell, photos)

BIBLIOGRAPHY

Atwater, Mrs. Isaac (Permelia A. Sanborn). *Pioneer Life in Minneapolis: From a Woman's Standpoint, 1840–1894.* Minneapolis: DeVeny Printing Company, 1894.

Balch-Tullis Artificial Limb Company, Manufacturers of Air Cushion Limbs. Catalog. Minneapolis: [company published], 1928.

Beltrami, Giacomo C. *A Pilgrimage in America: Leading to the Discovery of the Sources of the Mississippi and Bloody River: With a Description of the Whole Course of the Former and of the Ohio.* Chicago: Quadrangle Books, 1962.

Bliss, John H. "Reminiscences of Fort Snelling." *Minnesota Historical Society Collections* 6 (1894): 335–53.

Bremer, Fredrika. *The Homes of the New World: Impressions of America.* Translated by Mary Howitt. New York: Harper and Brothers, 1853.

Carver, Jonathan. *Travels through the Interior Parts of North America, in the Years 1766, 1767, and 1768.* London: C. Dilly, 1781.

Cathcart, Rebecca Marshall. "A Sheaf of Remembrances." *Minnesota Historical Society Collections* 15 (1909–14): 515–52.

Catlin, George. *Letters and Notes on the Manners, Customs, and Condition of the North American Indians.* New York: Wiley and Putnam, 1842.

Christian, Mary to "Sister Carrie," May 26, 1878. Edwin H. Brown and Family papers, Minnesota Historical Society.

Clark, Edwin. "Autobiography of Edwin Clark." Edwin Clark papers, Minnesota Historical Society.

Crocker, Betty. "Bisquick Fresh Cherry Cobbler." General Mills Test Kitchen radio transcript, July 1939. Leslie L. Anderson and Family papers, Minnesota Historical Society.

Dexter, Walter Ernest. Forest History Society, comp. Interviews with Pioneer Lumbermen. Minnesota Historical Society.

Edgar, William C. "The Miller and His Mill." *The Chautauquan.* Chautauqua, N.Y.: Chautauqua Press, 1892.

Ellet, Elizabeth F. *Summer Rambles in the West.* New York: J. C. Riker, 1853.

Featherstonhaugh, George. *A Canoe Voyage up the Minnay Sotor, With an Account of the Lead and Copper Deposits in Wisconsin, of the Gold Region in the Cherokee Country, and Sketches of Popular Manners.* Reprint edition. St. Paul: Minnesota Historical Society Press, 1970.

Forsyth, Thomas. "Fort Snelling: Col. Leavenworth's Expedition to Establish It, in 1819." *Minnesota Historical Society Collections* 3 (1870–80): 139–67.

Frank, Melvin L. "Sawmill City Boyhood." Manuscript collection, Minnesota Historical Society.

Fuller, Jane Gay. "From Our Correspondent of the Far West." (New York) *Evening Mirror,* February 16, 1855. Reprinted in Minnesota History 29 (1948): 29–35.

Gale, Harlow A. *Minneapolis: A Short Reversal of Human Thought. Being the Letters and Diary of Mr. Harlow A. Gale, 1857 to 1859.* Minneapolis: [privately printed], 1922.

Gay, Eva [pseud.]. "Workers in Wool." *St. Paul Globe,* May 20, 1888.

Granger, Sheridan. Interview by Julie Davis. Tape recording and transcript, October 5, 2001. Minnesota Historical Society.

Gray, W. D. "A Quarter-Century of Milling." *Northwestern Miller,* December 27, 1899.

Grey, Emily O. G. "The Black Community in Territorial St. Anthony: A Memoir." Edited by Patricia C. Harpole. *Minnesota History* 49 (1984): 42–53.

Griffith, Henry L. *Minneapolis: The New Sawdust Town.* Minneapolis: Bolger Publications, 1968.

Gyllstrom, Paul. "Notes on Early Minneapolis." Manuscript collection, Minnesota Historical Society.

Hamsun, Knut. "On the Prairie: A Sketch of the Red River Valley." *Minnesota History* 37 (1961): 265–70.

Hancock, H. B. to J. P. Russell and Huy, January 12, 1871. Manuscript collection, Hennepin History Museum, Minneapolis, Minnesota.

Hennepin, Louis. *Description of Louisiana, Newly Discovered to the Southwest of New France by Order of the King.* Translated from the original by Marion E. Cross. Minneapolis: University of Minnesota Press, 1980.

Hesler, Alexander to Russell Blakeley [n.d.]. Manuscript collection, Minnesota Historical Society.

Hinrichs, Don. Interview by Julie Davis. Tape recording and transcript, October 9, 2001. Minnesota Historical Society.

Hoag, Charles to editor, *St. Anthony Express,* November 5, 1852.

Hornicek, Louis. Interview by Paul Blankman. Tape recording and transcript, August 16, 2001. Minnesota Historical Society.

Ireland, John. Speech, quoted in *Minneapolis Tribune,* January 12, 1892.

Kohl, Johann Georg. "Johann Georg Kohl: A German Traveler in Minnesota Territory." Translated and edited by Frederic Trautmann. *Minnesota History* 49 (1984): 126–39.

Long, Stephen H. "Voyage in a Six-Oared Skiff to the Falls of St. Anthony in 1817." *Minnesota Historical Society Collections* 2 (1860–67): 7–88.

McCoy, John. "Reminiscences" [n.d.]. Manuscript collection, Minnesota Historical Society.

McFarlane, William K. "Sketch of Minnasota by an Emigrant." *Minnesota History* 7 (1926): 336–39.

McLinn, Dorothy. Interview by Julie Davis. Tape recording and transcript, October 23, 2001. Minnesota Historical Society.

Martin, Franklin. *The Joy of Living: An Autobiography.* Garden City, N.Y.: Doubleday, Doran, and Company, 1933.

Metcalf, Isaac to his wife, July 12, 1855, Letters of Isaac S. Metcalf, Minnesota Historical Society.

North, Ann to parents, December 9, 1849, North Papers, Henry E. Huntington Library and Art Gallery, San Marino, California.

Pardee, Walter Stone. Autobiography. Walter Stone Pardee papers, Minnesota Historical Society.

Patricelli, John ("Pat"). Interview by Julie Davis. Tape recording and transcript, October 1, 2001. Minnesota Historical Society.

Peckham, Stephen F. *The Dust Explosions at Minneapolis May 2, 1878, and Other Dust Explosions.* New York: [n.p.], 1908.

Prescott, Philander. "Autobiography and Reminiscences of Philander Prescott." *Minnesota Historical Society Collections* 6 (1894): 475–91.

Schatzel, G. W. "Among the Wheat-Fields of Minnesota." *Harper's New Monthly Magazine* 36 (1868): 190–201. Reprinted in *With Various Voices: Recordings of North Star Life*, edited by Theodore C. Blegen and Philip D. Jordan. St. Paul: Itasca Press, 1949.

Schoolcraft, Henry Rowe. *Narrative Journal of Travels through the Northwestern Regions of the United States.* Albany: E. and E. Hosford, 1821.

Smalley, Eugene V. "The Flour-Mills of Minneapolis." *Century Illustrated Monthly Magazine,* 32.5 (1886): 37–47.

Smith, Charles C. "Stone Railway Viaduct Across the Mississippi River at Minneapolis Built during 1882 and 1883." Manuscript collection, Minnesota Historical Society.

Snelling, Josiah to Thomas Jesup, August 16, 1824. Fort Snelling Consolidated Correspondence File, Office of the Quartermaster General, National Archives, record group 92.

Spielman, Jean E. *The Intricacies of the Wheat Pit.* Minneapolis: Flour and Cereal Mill Workers Local Union No. 92 and Grain Elevator Workers Local Union No. 160, 1920.

Stanchfield, Daniel. "History of Pioneer Lumbering on the Upper Mississippi and Its Tributaries, with Biographical Sketches." *Minnesota Historical Society Collections* 9 (1901): 325–62.

Stevens, John H. "Valedictory of Col. J. H. Stevens." *St. Anthony Express,* January 13, 1855.

Tyra, Joseph W. Interview by Jay Edgerton. Tape recording and transcript, June 9, 1958. International Multifoods Corporation Records. Minnesota Historical Society.

Viator [pseud.], "Impressions of Minnesota Territory by a Pennsylvania Visitor of 1857." *Venango Spectator* (Pennsylvania), 1857. Reprinted in *Minnesota History* 46 (1979): 210–27.

Watt, Robert. "A Danish Visitor of the Seventies." Translated and edited by Jacob Hodnefield. *Minnesota History* 10 (1929): 409–24.

Welles, Henry T. *Autobiography and Reminiscences.* Minneapolis: [privately printed], 1899.

Wells, Frank. "Journey to Minneapolis." Manuscript collection, Hennepin History Museum, Minneapolis, Minnesota.

Wilkinson, Francis. "Here and There in America: Adventures and Observations of a Craven Lad." *West Yorkshire Pioneer* (Skipton, England), March 1869. Reprinted in Minnesota History 27 (1946): 283–99.

Witchie, Edward E. Speech, 1877. Manuscript collection, Hennepin History Museum, Minneapolis, Minnesota.

Woods, Charles Henry to Gilman Henry Tucker, July 26, 1866. "A Letter from Minneapolis." *Hennepin History* 50.1 (1991): 23–26.

Woodward, Mary Dodge. *The Checkered Years: A Bonanza Farm Diary, 1884–1888.* St. Paul: Minnesota Historical Society Press, 1989.

INDEX